Homer's two great epic poems, the *Iliad* and the *Odyssey*, stand as cornerstones not only of Western literature but also of Western thought and culture, for although readers of two millennia have imitated or opposed these works' paradigm of character and action, few have ignored it. Where the *Iliad* strikes a heavy tone of tragic grandeur, the *Odyssey* evokes an atmosphere of adventure and fate. The latter work's key figure, Odysseus the restless wanderer, pervades our language and our thinking: his self-defining journey of experience and maturation has remained one of the world's most explored subjects of artistic expression.

In his cogent reading of the *Odyssey* William G. Thalmann argues that, like its hero, the text is impossible to reduce to a single summary or set of oppositions. As presented in Homer's narrative, the polarities of nature versus civilization, war versus peace, action versus word, and force versus *metis* (intelligence) are fraught with ambiguity. Thalmann singles out in particular the precarious nature of *metis*, which imbues Odysseus with constructive intelligence but also a dangerous duplicity. Similarly, Thalmann contends that in all his travels Odysseus both inflicts pain and himself suffers after having saved his own life via his cleverness.

Aside from its explorations of human character, however, the poem quite simply tells a wonderful story. Odysseus's myriad adventures during his 10-year struggle to get home to Ithaka have the powerful appeal of folktale and fairy tale: the poem's narrative, Thalmann asserts, offers the pleasure of desiring an end that is delayed by obstacles in the outer world and the necessity for intrigues on Ithaka, with the simultaneous assurance that the end will come, and that it will be a happy one.

Thalmann perceptively identifies traces of class and gender inquiry in Homer's epic. The poem seems to open up questions about the upholding of a system by which those at the top of society are maintained by the labor of those below, Thalmann maintains; in due course, however, these questions are closed off with the ideal solution of the return of the righteous king, promising prosperity for all. Additionally, Thalmann detects in Penelope an independence and importance rarely accorded women in Greek literature or Greek life; her like-mindedness with Odysseus is emphasized and their marriage characterized as a collaboration between them.

What makes Homer's text so relevant to our times, Thalmann concludes, is its suffusion with contradiction and elusiveness. Odysseus, after all, is a hero with a constantly

(Continued on back flap)

The Odyssey
an epic of return

❡

Twayne's Masterwork Studies
Robert Lecker, General Editor

The Odyssey
an epic of return

❡

William G. Thalmann

Twayne Publishers • New York

Maxwell Macmillan Canada • Toronto

Maxwell Macmillan International • New York Oxford Singapore Sydney

Twayne's Masterwork Studies No. 100

Copyright 1992 by Twayne Publishers

Twayne Publishers
Macmillan Publishing Company
866 Third Avenue
New York, New York 10022

Maxwell Macmillan Canada, Inc.
1200 Eglinton Avenue East
Suite 200
Don Mills, Ontario M3C 3N1

Macmillan Publishing Company is a part of the Maxwell Communication Group of Companies.

Library of Congress Cataloging-in-Publication Data
Thalmann, William G., 1947–
The Odyssey : an epic of return / William G. Thalmann.
p. cm. — (Twayne's masterwork studies ; 100)
Includes bibliographical references and index.
ISBN 0-8057-9424-7 — ISBN 0-8057-8564-7 (pbk.)
1. Homer. Odyssey. 2. Epic poetry, Greek—History and criticism. 3. Odysseus (Greek mythology) in literature. 4. Return in literature. I. Title. II. Series: Twayne's masterwork studies ; no. 99.
PA4167.T45 1992
883'.01—dc20   92-11677
                                              CIP

10 9 8 7 6 5 4 3 2 1 (alk. paper)

10 9 8 7 6 5 4 3 2 1 (pbk.: alk. paper)

Printed in the United States of America.

contents

note on the references vii
acknowledgments ix
chronology xi

LITERARY AND HISTORICAL CONTEXT

1. The Eighth-Century Renaissance   3
2. The Importance of the Work   9
3. Critical Reception   15

A READING

4. The Hero Absent: Books 1–4   31
5. The Hero in Transition: Books 5–8   47
6. The Hero Wandering: Books 9–12   65
7. The Hero Returned: Books 13–24   95
8. Poetry in the *Odyssey*   125
9. Unraveling the Web   133

notes   139
bibliography   143
index   147

note on the references

Readers will not find in this study systematic discussion of the heavily formulaic nature of Homeric poetry, the oral poetic tradition that seems to lie behind it, the question of whether the poems were composed orally or with the aid of writing, or the transmission of the text. Although I consider these issues important and have taken them carefully into account in thinking about the *Iliad* and the *Odyssey*, discussing each would require a great amount of space. I have instead concentrated on a literary reading of the *Odyssey*, letting these concerns come into play where they seemed to matter especially. Excellent and accessible treatments of these issues can be found in the studies by Jasper Griffin and Mark Edwards, listed in the Bibliography.

This book is based on and quotes from Robert Fitzgerald's 1961 translation of the *Odyssey*. Although the most recent (1990) edition of Fitzgerald has line numbers, they are not those of the original Greek text; thus I have used a dual reference system. I cite page numbers (which are the same for all paperback editions of the Fitzgerald text) preceded by book and line numbers of the Greek text, thereby enabling readers using other translations—including Richmond Lattimore's—to locate the passages in question. For example: "20.149–54, p. 379" means lines 149–54 of Book 20, which will be found on page 379 of Fitzgerald's translation.

Fitzgerald transliterates Greek proper names directly instead of giving the Latin forms of these names, which in many cases are more familiar to English-speaking readers: for example, "Akhilleus" rather than "Achilles," "Telemakhos" rather than "Telemachus," "Ithaka" instead of "Ithaca." I have generally followed his practice, even though "Kyklops" will look strange at first to those familiar with the Cyclops. My motive was neither consistency with Fitzgerald nor (I hope) pedantry; I wanted to guide the reader to hear these names approximately as Homer's audience did, and to hear in this small way something of the sound of his language and his poetry. If the result is to de-familiarize the poem somewhat, there is no harm in that.

acknowledgments

Quotations from Robert Fitzgerald's *Homer: The Odyssey* are reprinted by permission of Vintage Books, a division of Random House, Inc. Copyright © 1961, 1962 by Robert Fitzgerald, © renewed 1989 by Benedict R. C. Fitzgerald.

Chapter 8, "Poetry in the *Odyssey*," presents briefly some ideas in a chapter by the same title in my *Conventions of Form and Thought in Early Greek Epic Poetry* (Baltimore and London: Johns Hopkins University Press, 1984).

The frontispiece photograph is reproduced courtesy of the J. Paul Getty Museum, Malibu, California.

❡

It is a pleasure to thank my wife, Susan, and my colleagues Carolyn Dewald and Martha Malamud for carefully reading this book in manuscript and giving me the benefit of their shrewd and detailed advice. I would also like to thank the series editor, Robert Lecker, and the editorial staff at Twayne Publishers for their help and good sense. My children Sarah and Christopher, always fascinated with the story of Odysseus, took great interest in the writing of the book. I hope that they someday come to share my own perpetual delight in the *Odyssey* itself.

Statuette group: lyre-player and boy. Bronze, 11.5 cm. Early seventh century B.C. Collection of the J. Paul Getty Museum, Malibu, California.

chronology

All dates are B.C. and approximate.

1325–1200   The prosperity and power of Mycenaean civilization are at their height: the "Late Helladic IIIB" period.

1225   Troy VIIA is sacked, which may be the historical basis for the story of the Trojan War. If so, fiction has exercised its privilege and exaggerated the wealth of Troy in this phase and the war's magnitude.

1200   Violent destruction of Mycenaean palaces.

1200–1100   Decline of Mycenaean culture.

1100–750   Dark Age: population and material culture decline steeply from 1200 to 1050.

1100–1000   Traditional date of the Dorian Invasion.

1050   Iron begins to be used widely in Greece. Protogeometric pottery appears.

1050–950   Large-scale migration to the Aegean islands and the coast of Asia Minor.

900–750   Geometric period, so called from its characteristic pottery style, which goes through several phases.

750   By this time the alphabet has appeared in Greece.

750–700   Late geometric period, the eighth-century renaissance. Population rises sharply, farming intensifies, the polis takes form, sites in Italy and Sicily are colonized, trade and crafts blossom, and temples begin to be constructed. The *Iliad* and *Odyssey* are composed, whether by the same or different poets is unknown.

700–480   Archaic Age.

479–323   Classical period.

323–31   Hellenistic period: texts of the Homeric epics are edited by scholars at the library in Alexandria.

Literary and Historical Context

❡

1

The Eighth-Century Renaissance

The *Iliad* and the *Odyssey* look back some five centuries to the Trojan War, fought (if it actually occurred) toward the end of the Mycenaean period. This was a time of extraordinary cultural achievement, wealth, and military power on the Greek mainland. In each area authority was centered on a palace within a strongly fortified citadel. There a king ruled through an extensive civil and military bureaucracy over the villages and farmlands in his district.

For reasons now unknown, this age came to an end between 1200 and 1100 B.C. with the violent destruction and abandonment of many Mycenaean centers. There followed a period now called the Dark Age, which later Greeks associated with the invasion southward of Dorians from the Northwest and migration from the mainland to the coast of Asia Minor. Much about this period remains obscure, including the historicity of the "Dorian Invasion." It is clear, however, that population and material culture declined steeply. Around 1050, with the widespread adoption of iron rather than bronze and the appearance of a new type of pottery ("protogeometric"), a process of slow improvement began that continued through the tenth and ninth centuries.

All the more remarkable by contrast are the rapid and interrelated developments that occurred in the eighth century, particularly in the second half (750–700). Those 50 years concern us especially, for within them the *Iliad* and (somewhat later) the *Odyssey* were probably composed. But the Homeric epics were just one significant aspect of what has been called the eighth-century renaissance. By 700 there had appeared in some form the institutions and structures that were basic to the often-brilliant developments of the Archaic Age and to the second cultural explosion at its end, the "classical" civilization of the fifth century.[1]

Perhaps the most fundamental development was a dramatic rise in population that began around 750 and leveled off around 700 (Snodgrass, 23–25). At the same time, doubtless because of this increase, in many places adjacent villages grew together near a hill that would serve for defense in case of attack, and the basis was formed of that characteristic Greek political unit, the polis (plural *poleis*). This word, inadequately translated "city-state," designated the combination in political unity of an urban center, with its acropolis, and the surrounding countryside, with its farms and villages. For centuries afterward large parts of Greece were occupied by these independent poleis, with no overarching political unity, and the development of Greek thought and culture was profoundly influenced by this form of political organization. The heart of the polis in the eighth century, however, was little more than a town: a cluster of houses, and on or near the acropolis an agora, or assembly place (only later, with the progress of crafts and trade, did this word come to mean "marketplace"). Near the agora might be the relatively imposing house of the leading nobleman.[2]

More people meant greater need for food. Arable farming was intensified and new lands cleared, but increasing pressure on available land resulted in colonization, in the eighth century notably in Italy and Sicily, and hence an expansion of cultural horizons. The growth of trade also produced this expansion. The rise in population made specialization possible, and various crafts developed (we shall see significant references in the *Odyssey* to shipbuilding, for instance). Crafts in turn led to a demand for raw materials not found in Greece, and hence to trade (Coldstream, 368). The Phoinikians, who figure in the *Odyssey*, were the leading traders in the Mediterranean, and so possibly the main transmitters of Eastern culture to Greece, but Greek merchants must also have been active. The earliest colony in the West, Pithekoussai on the island of Ischia off the northern tip of the Bay of Naples, was evidently founded to trade with the Etruscans for their iron ore. The increase at this time in metallic votive dedications in religious

4

sanctuaries testifies to a renewal of trade, interrupted during the Dark Age, in copper and tin, which were necessary for bronze (Snodgrass, 52–55).

The number of sanctuaries active in this period and the larger volume of all offerings in them imply a rise in religious as well as economic activity. Most significant in itself and in light of later developments is that the earliest known temples date from the late eighth century. A temple would have been a collective enterprise by the polis, and both the building and the cult expressed and fostered a self-conscious communal identity. At the same time, certain sanctuaries not identified with a specific polis were taking on a Panhellenic significance that united the Greeks culturally despite their political fragmentation (Snodgrass, 55–62; Coldstream, 338–39). Examples are Apollo's oracle at Delphi, Olympia, where the great games were instituted, according to the traditional date, in 776, and Delos, where Apollo and Artemis were born beneath the date palm mentioned by Odysseus to Nausikaa (6.162, pp. 103–4).

In two further developments skills lost since the collapse of Mycenaean civilization were revived in very different form. First, vase painting reveals a growing interest in pictorial representation, especially of the human form. Men and women appear not for their own sake, however, but as part of scenes, such as battles and funerals—many of them generic, no doubt, but some perhaps intended to tell a particular story (Snodgrass, 65–77). Second, literacy was recovered. The Mycenaeans had a form of writing, but it was a cumbersome syllabary (each symbol stood for a syllable, not a separate sound) used only, as far as we know, by palace scribes to keep inventories. Whether others could read and write, or needed to, is unknown. This writing vanished with the palaces. But sometime before 750, after centuries of illiteracy, the Greeks adapted the Phoinikian alphabet, to which they added the signs for vowels with which the Phoinikians had not bothered. This alphabet, easy to learn and to use, was potentially much more than a means for bureaucrats to wield power. How widely and how fast literacy spread in the eighth century is, again, unknown, but eventually writing had profound effects on everything from the polis, whose laws, inscribed on stone, could be publicly displayed, and literature, since texts could be preserved by means other than oral transmission and memory, to the Greek mentality in general.

All these changes and especially the growing prosperity inevitably sharpened the distinction between the common people and the aristocrats (in the Dark Age, when the way of life was uniformly depressed, this distinction was probably small). In particular, the aristocracy evidently became increasingly conscious of itself as a class. The cost will have been social tension, between high and low and also among the powerful.

In contrast with the Mycenaean palaces ruled by kings, the highest political unit throughout most of Greece in the Dark Age was the village, or district. Within it, many scholars think, was a loose tribal organization of clans, the heads of which wielded power locally. One of these men might have enjoyed a more or less formal preeminence, taking the lead in war, settling quarrels, and seeing that religious observances were carried out. Both these rulers and the other chieftains who were virtually their peers can be called *basilees* (in later Greek, "kings," but surely something less exalted in this period) in our early poetic texts.

The coalescence into the polis brought a need for a more complex central authority. For a time, rule by a single preeminent person may have continued in this larger unit; he would have conducted affairs after discussion with the other nobles in the agora, perhaps in the presence of the common people (an example might be Alkinoos and his 12 nobles in the *Odyssey*). But the nobles could also vie for power with their chief. By the end of the eighth century, single rule over the polis had disappeared from most parts of Greece.[3] It was replaced by the authority in each polis of a few aristocratic families or a single family. Where the title *basileus* lingered, it now referred to a magistracy held by aristocrats, as all offices were in a new and more effective centralization of power. In the seventh and sixth centuries those aristocracies that abused their power were replaced by tyrants, who took up the popular cause against the nobles and represented a short-lived return to single rule.

Amid all the changes, so important for the future, the eighth century shows signs of interest in the Mycenaean past as an age of heroes. Offerings were left in Mycenaean tombs whose occupants' names were no longer known; it was felt, nevertheless, that the power of *some* hero still resided in these tombs. Separate cults of heroes known from saga, and named in Homer, also sprang up, among them Menelaos and Helen at Therapne near Sparta and Odysseus himself, who was worshiped as a hero in a cave beside Polis Bay on Ithaka. In addition, some aristocratic burials seem to imitate funerals described in epic poetry, as do depictions of funerals on monumental (and expensive) vases found in aristocratic tombs. And some vase paintings seem to recall the heroic age either through certain details or through reference to stories of heroes' exploits (Coldstream, 341–57). Obviously this pride in the past promoted the interests of aristocrats, who often claimed descent from the heroes. But for everyone, the heroic stories, the possession of a history, must have provided both inspiration and a new sense of cultural identity (Snodgrass, 77–78).[4]

The Homeric epics were a symptom of this interest and of the cultural revival generally; they were also a stimulus to further development. A long tradition of oral narrative poetry seems to lie behind them; one important piece of evidence for this tradition is the formulaic nature of the epics' language and especially the systematic character of the formulas, features best explained as aids to oral composition. But the *Iliad* and *Odyssey* represent something new, not only in their quality but also in their monumental scale. The epics that preceded them, all now lost, must have been far shorter and less ambitious. Whether the new technology of writing played a role in their composition and preservation and, if so, what role is still much debated. In any case these poems are fitting expressions of the eighth century's innovative spirit, and their influence on later Greek culture was massive.

The poems' relation to the culture that produced them is complex, however. The society depicted within the poems is composite. Especially in the *Iliad* there are some genuine reminiscences of Mycenaean society, in some cases references to objects far earlier than the time of the Trojan War. Presumably memory of these, along with the stories themselves, would have been kept alive by the oral poetic tradition. There are also some Dark Age elements, including, perhaps, the social structure on Ithaka.[5] And there are undoubtedly eighth-century elements, such as the Phaiakians' polis. Its founding, with the building of walls and houses and the distribution of land (6.7–10, p. 99), seems to echo the activity of contemporary colonists in the West. Odysseus looks at the uninhabited island off the Kyklopes' land in Book 9 through what surely are a colonist's eyes. And the stories of his wanderings may owe much to tales brought back by contemporary merchants and other travelers from distant parts.

The poems' links to their contemporary society, however, must go beyond simply reproducing certain aspects. These texts, whether written or not, were not read privately but performed, sometimes in aristocratic houses but probably also in other settings before popular audiences. No matter what the age of this or that object or practice described in the poems, their narratives cannot have been of purely antiquarian interest. These heroic stories were also ways of exploring current questions and conflicts. That is, the poems were deeply implicated in the social and political issues of their time. At this distance we can form only an approximate picture of the nature of their involvement; some suggestions are given in the final chapter of this book.

2

The Importance of the Work

Although the *Odyssey* should be read within its historical setting, it long survived the circumstances that produced it and still speaks to us across nearly three millennia. What accounts for this continuing power? Why has the poem seemed at various periods—why does it still seem—more than a mere relic of the past?

Part of the answer is that the *Odyssey* and the *Iliad* became the Greeks' most essential cultural documents, offering paradigms of character and action to be imitated or opposed but never ignored. And since Greek culture is an integral part of our own, the *Odyssey* is at the very root of our tradition. The poem's place in literary history is a specific manifestation of this broader significance. It not only stimulated and influenced an array of later texts in various genres; it also, along with the *Iliad*, set once and for all the rules and conventions of the epic. Artists from Virgil through Milton to James Joyce drew on a genre established for them by the Homeric poems.

To make these statements is, however, to beg the question: Through what intrinsic qualities does the *Odyssey* merit this stature? The answer has to begin with the source of every reader's pleasure in this text: the poem tells a wonderful story. Here we have a wrong desperately in need of righting—chaos on Ithaka and within Odysseus's house, the suitors in possession, the wife's position precarious, the son chafing at his exclusion from his patrimony. The returned Odysseus wreaks a satisfyingly gory revenge on the usurpers, and home and society are harmoniously reintegrated. One part of us, at least—our urge for clarity and order—responds deeply to the rhythm of this story. Another, contradictory impulse—the pleasure we take in adventure—opens us to the enjoyment of Odysseus's wanderings before he reaches Ithaka: his encounters with beings outside humanity's normal range, the excitement of the dangers he faces, and the ways he gets through them. Odysseus's adventures have the powerful appeal of folktale and fairy tale; from an early age children continue to be fascinated by them in prose paraphrases. The poem's narrative, then, offers the pleasure of desiring an end that is delayed by obstacles in the outer world and the necessity for intrigues on Ithaka, with the simultaneous assurance that the end will come, and that it will be happy.

It is easy to see Odysseus's adventures as the essence of the poem. Odysseus as a restless wanderer, an odyssey as a journey of experience and maturation—these have entered our language and our thinking. They are, we say, part of our tradition, our heritage from the Greeks.

If the wanderings are kept in perspective, however, we can see something else the *Odyssey* offers, of even more importance. The poem does offer episodes of unmatched excitement, but those adventures occupy only four books (9–12) out of 24 and need to be read in context. For fully half the poem (Books 13–24) Odysseus is at home on his native island, Ithaka. Throughout all his experience in worlds known and unknown, Odysseus wants only one thing: to get home. Kalypso offers him eternal ease in ageless immortality, and yet he leaves her for the aging Penelope, the harder life on Ithaka, and eventual death. To remain in a state of timeless pleasure or to die on the journey as his companions do is, as the text repeats, to lose one's homecoming. Home is the controlling value in this poem.

The homecoming must be achieved, both by the hero who surmounts obstacles in the outer world and on Ithaka and by those at home who have remained loyal to him. To depict a homecoming, especially from the Trojan War, as a heroic exploit might seem to suggest an odd view of heroism. Akhilleus, the hero of the *Iliad*, gained honor and fame at the cost of an early though glorious death in battle. The *Odyssey*, by contrast, is a poem of survival, the triumph of life over death both in glory on the battlefield and alone in unknown parts and in life's continuation into old age in community with others. And if it has all the excitement of the dangers and difficulties of coming home, it also celebrates the decorum of ordinary life, down to the smallest details, in a way that would be unthinkable in the *Iliad* or most other heroic poetry:

> Eurykleia . . . called to the maids:
> "Bestir yourselves! you have your brooms, go sprinkle
> the rooms and sweep them, robe the chairs in red,
> sponge off the tables till they shine.
> Wash out the winebowls and two-handled cups.
> You others go fetch water from the spring."
> (20.149–54, p. 379)

The heroes in the *Iliad* probably need their rooms swept too, but it is never mentioned. The *Odyssey*, through such details and other effects, builds a picture of life in a well-ordered household and city as the goal finally achieved by Odysseus's restoration to his home. Odysseus's experiences during his 20-year absence—his encounters with warfare, nature, the monstrous, the magical, the divine, the human in distorted or exaggerated form—all define by contrast familiar human civilization and reveal its value.

Odysseus understands that value when he declines immortality as well as when he surmounts other temptations and obstacles. The paradox that this hero of the very broadest possible experience wants only home and family is resolved when we realize that the poem offers not a lament for the failures and vulnerabilities of human life (though it recognizes these) but a vision of what can be achieved positively by recognizing and embracing the necessities that go with being mortal: toil, old age, and death. It teaches the value of relationships, of participation in family and community, not only as defense against the uncertainties of life but also as the realization of what it means to be fully human, rather than either a god or a brute monster. This vision, achieved by struggle, is complex, mature, and sophisticated.

Odysseus's qualities, essential to conveying this vision, are as comprehensive as the plot of his poem. The first line of the *Odyssey* describes him as *polutropos* (a word used one other time in the poem, again of Odysseus): "of many turnings," evidently in two

11

senses. First, Odysseus has "turned" much throughout the world, has roamed widely. But, second, he also is a man of many mental twists and turns, clever and cunning. And so the word sums up both Odysseus's fate of physical wandering before reaching home and the intellectual quality by which he overcomes danger and delay (Fitzgerald thus translates the word twice: "that man skilled in all ways of contending, / the wanderer"). Two other adjectives often applied to him in the text correspond, respectively, to one of these meanings. Odysseus is *polutlas*, "much enduring"—a reference to his toils and suffering and also to the physical and mental endurance that carries him through (think of him clinging to the fig tree for an afternoon as he dangles above Kharybdis). But he is also *polumêtis*, "of much *metis*" (intelligence, cleverness). *Metis* is Odysseus's outstanding quality, and it is constantly opposed in the poem to physical force; it is, for example, his weapon against the Kyklops and the numerically superior suitors. It is a quality peculiar to culture and as such is opposed to the brute force of nature. It also implies an opposition between the external world and the individual's inner thoughts and feelings, between appearance and reality. *Metis* is the quality that enables Odysseus to face a hostile world with his inner resources, to manipulate appearances and disguise the truth of situations.[6] Wandering, sufferings, and cleverness: Odysseus has these in abundance, as the prefix *polu-* (much) in all these epithets indicates. This polytropic hero labors and plots on a grand scale. He is a hero of culture, and in the end the poem convinces us that he, if anyone, both deserves his homecoming and can appreciate it.

Odysseus, then, is at times an active manipulator shaping his own fate and at other times a passive victim of forces—such as Poseidon's anger—beyond any mortal's control. His character is the site of "a vigorous and unstable dialectic between the ability actively to engage and transform the world and the passive subjection to its unalterable necessities."[7] Through his story the poem holds in balance two opposed views of the world, as hemming in human freedom in favor of tragic outcomes and as open to being molded by mortals for the fulfillment of their desires. If the poem's conclusion seems mainly happy, we should not forget that its hero had to wander for 10 years and must someday die.

In these and other ways the text reveals important ambiguities in its dominant values and in Odysseus's character, and we need to be attentive to them. Thus the *Odyssey* continues to raise questions about human civilization even while celebrating it. With these implied questions, as well as by playing adventure off against the stability of home, the poem challenges us to decide what truly is important, what constitutes the good life and what we must do to achieve it.

The *Odyssey* has not always been read in this way, however. Readers have viewed it differently in successive ages. They have found in it what they looked for, and that was in large part a function of the concerns and experiences of their times. This openness to the unfolding of ever-new interpretations, the ability to satisfy people's changing needs and interests through time, is perhaps *the* defining characteristic of a poetic masterpiece.

3

Critical Reception

It would be impossible to overstate Homer's influence on subsequent Greek culture.[8] In later antiquity he could be referred to simply as "the Poet," without ambiguity. Homer and Hesiod, wrote the historian Herodotus in the fifth century B.C., "created a theogony [account of the gods' origins] for the Greeks, gave the gods their titles and epithets, distinguished their functions and skills, and indicated their forms." Whatever the literal truth of this statement, Homer, along with Hesiod, clearly shaped and maintained the Greeks' heritage and helped provide them with a Panhellenic culture that was a counterweight to their political fragmentation into "city-states." The sixth-century B.C. poet and philosopher Xenophanes said that "from the beginning all have learned from Homer." They did so, evidently, not so much from reading the poems as from hearing them performed by *rhapsodes*, itinerant reciters and perhaps interpreters of Homeric and other poetry (Plato gives a splendid though unsympathetic portrait of a rhapsode in his dialogue *Ion*). From the sixth century B.C. on, the Homeric epics were recited by relays of rhapsodes at the annual Panathenaic Festival in Athens, and similar performances may have occurred from earlier times at the great Ionian festivals at Delos and Mykale. On such occasions the poems were accessible to mass audiences. They were also studied in the more restricted setting of Athenian schools. One way or another, Greeks seem to have grown up with an intimate knowledge of these poems.

15

We know of no ancient Greek literary work modeled on the *Odyssey* or even on an episode of it (except for Euripides's satyr play *Kyklops* and—distantly—Theocritus's eleventh idyll). The poem's influence was more subtle. Lyric poets of the seventh and sixth centuries B.C., with the *Odyssey* apparently in mind, several times praise such Odyssean qualities as versatility and steadfastness and oppose them to mere appearance. In the fifth century, however, these very qualities came to be regarded as amoral and ruthless—hence dangerous—and Odysseus was viewed with hostility. Pindar attributed Odysseus's defeat of Aias in the (non-Homeric) contest for Akhilleus's arms to his wily lies, which proved more effective than Aias's heroic deeds in battle. Pindar here displays his aristocratic bias; the democratically inspired Athenian tragedy at first offers a contrast. Dramatizing the same story in his *Ajax* in the 440s B.C., the heyday of Athenian achievement and confidence, Sophocles portrayed Odysseus as humane and temperate toward his adversary. His Odysseus seems to embody Athenian civic virtues, as opposed to Aias's egotism, traditionally heroic but self-destructive and obsolete under contemporary political conditions.

Athens would soon learn, however, the consequences of divorcing appearance from reality, of politicians' manipulating language for personal advancement, in the demoralization that accompanied the Peloponnesian War, and some 30 years later, in his *Philoktetes* (409 B.C.), Sophocles gave a very different view of Odysseus. Seeking to enlist Akhilleus's son Neoptolemos in a heartless deception to bring Philoktetes and his bow to Troy, Odysseus urges, "Give yourself to me for shamelessness for one short day, and then be called the most reverent of mortals for the rest of time." But Odysseus had already appeared as a cynical stage villain in Euripides's *Hekabe* in the 420s. In the aftermath of Troy's fall, the shade of Akhilleus has demanded that Polyxena, daughter of the Trojan queen Hekabe, be sacrificed to him. Odysseus justifies the sacrifice to Hekabe, who earlier saved his life, on the grounds that it is in the state's interest to reward its heroes. Thus in the late fifth century the Homeric Odysseus's concern for the community's good had become a ruthless political expediency, ready to excuse anything on the grounds of "national security."

Although all these post-Homeric portrayals of Odysseus are based on qualities found in Homer's hero, they all emphasize one aspect of him and ignore others. And so they sacrifice the complexity and balance of Homer's portrayal. In addition, different views of Odysseus are adopted according to each era's concerns and values. These tendencies—to simplify and to interpret in light of contemporary conditions—characterized most of the remaining history of responses to the *Odyssey*.

Besides literary successors, Homer also had detractors among the Greeks. The fourth-century B.C. Cynic philosopher Zoilos so ferociously criticized Homer's characters and fantastic incidents that he earned the nickname "scourge of Homer," and his name became a byword for captious criticism. Earlier, Xenophanes, who evidently did not think it a good thing that everyone learned from Homer, said in a poem, "Homer and Hesiod attributed to the gods everything / that earns reproaches and blame from mortals: / theft, adultery, and mutual deceptions." This charge is devastating because it is undeniable.

One way of defending Homer was to deny the importance of his text's literal meaning and to interpret him allegorically. This method began not long after Xenophanes and was later taken up by Stoic philosophers, who, along with Cynics, admired Odysseus's rationality, self-sufficiency, and devotion to communal welfare. Aristotle, on the other hand, met criticisms of alleged implausibility and inconsistencies directly in his *Homeric Problems*. In his *Poetics* he also praised the *Iliad* and *Odyssey* for their organic unity.

So far Homer belonged to general audiences and philosophers. The poems became the object of scholarship during its first efflorescence at Alexandria in Egypt during the third and second centuries B.C. The labors of a series of scholars, culminating in the work of Aristarchus around the middle of the second century, established, from among widely varying copies that seem to have been circulating previously, a standard text of the *Iliad* and *Odyssey* that is the distant ancestor of the medieval manuscripts that have come down to us. In addition, several scholars wrote explications of various aspects of both poems, including elucidations of rare or obsolete words and *Homeric Problems* in the tradition of Aristotle. Extracts were later made of these works, and these formed the basis of the marginal notes, or scholia, in surviving manuscripts to which we owe our knowledge of Alexandrian scholars' editorial and critical opinions. These scholars were concerned not only with deciding among variant readings but also with marking as interpolations passages that repeated or contradicted what was said elsewhere in each poem, and with explaining or emending away details of Homeric manners that offended sensibilities shaped by association with the royal court in Egypt (such as Nestor's daughter bathing Telemakhos in Book 3 of the *Odyssey*).

The *Odyssey* became widely accessible to the Romans early in their literary development, with its translation (or adaptation) into Latin by Livius Andronicus in the third century B.C. The most striking artistic response came from Virgil, who modeled much of the first half of his epic, the *Aeneid*, on Odysseus's wanderings and often echoes Homeric phrases. In his picture of Odysseus, or—his Latin name—Ulysses (Book 2), Virgil draws not on Homer but on the later view of the hero as a smooth and unscrupulous liar, but he characteristically complicates this tradition by presenting it in a lying story told by the treacherous Sinon. In general the Romans both condemned Odysseus and felt the Stoics' admiration for his other qualities. Typical of this schizophrenic attitude was the Stoic Seneca, who in his prose works commended Odysseus but in his tragedy *Trojan Women* followed—and passed on to later European dramatists—Euripides's portrayal of him as a villain.

A famous and influential comparison between the *Iliad* and the *Odyssey*—to the latter's detriment—was made in a treatise, probably of the first century A.D., falsely ascribed to Longinus and entitled *On the Sublime*. The *Iliad*, notes the author, is full of action and conflict; the *Odyssey* is more concerned with narrative, fanciful stories, and the depiction of character. From this difference it is inferred that Homer composed the *Odyssey* in his old age:

> In the *Odyssey* Homer may be likened to a sinking sun, whose grandeur remains without its intensity. He does not in the *Odyssey* maintain so high a pitch as in those poems of Ilium. His sublimities are not evenly sustained and free from the liability to sink; there is not the same profusion of accumulated passions, nor the supple and oratorical style, packed with images drawn from real life. You seem to see . . . the ebb and flow of greatness, and a fancy roving in the fabulous and incredible, as though the ocean were withdrawing into itself and were being laid bare within its own confines. (*On the Sublime*, 9.13)[9]

18

The writer still admires the *Odyssey* ("if I speak of old age, it is nevertheless the old age of Homer"), but the tendency to find it overshadowed by the *Iliad* has unfortunately been repeated by many readers. It is necessary to remember what standards are being applied. The essay seeks to describe the sublime and measure various kinds of style by it, and the evaluation of the Homeric epics accords with the general statement made later that "passion is as intimately allied with sublimity as sketches of character with entertainment" (*On the Sublime*, 29.2, p. 117). If we recognize this interest, we can still say that this writer has pointed to important differences between the two poems, without accepting the writer's relegation of the *Odyssey* to second place or the essay's biographical speculation.

Toward the end of the first century A.D. a fashion set in of disparaging Homer for not telling the truth about the Trojan War, and it was in this environment that sometime in the succeeding centuries two Latin works, allegedly eyewitness accounts of the war, became current, one purporting to be the journal kept by Dictys of Krete on the Akhaian side, the other supposedly written by Dares, a Phrygian and hence a Trojan ally. Both works focus on the war itself; a brief version of Odysseus's wanderings, with considerable departures from the *Odyssey*'s narrative, comes at the end of "Dictys's" work. The significance of these documents for us is that, with the disappearance of Greek learning from the West and until manuscripts of Homer were brought there again in the late fourteenth century, they were what Europe knew of the Trojan stories (they spawned a series of medieval Troy romances). During this time, however, one of the most magnificent re-creations of Odysseus in Western literature appeared: Dante's Ulysses, in Canto 26 of the *Inferno*.

Ulysses is punished in the circle of fraudulent counselors in the lower part of Hell by being completely enclosed, with Diomedes, in flame. He cannot speak directly, but in an inversion of the Pentecost story in Chapter 2 of *Acts of the Apostles*, his words must pass to the peak of the flame and set this "tongue" vibrating. In this way he tells his story. After he left Kirke, he says, his feelings for father, son, and wife were overcome by "the longing that I had to gain experience of the world, and of human vice and worth." And so he persuaded his crew to sail beyond the Strait of Gibraltar into the

Atlantic Ocean: "'O brothers,'" I said, 'who through a hundred thousand dangers have reached the west, to this so brief vigil of our senses that remains to us, choose not to deny experience, following the sun, of the world that has no people. Consider your origin: you were not made to live as brutes, but to pursue virtue and knowledge.'"[10] They journeyed to the Southern Hemisphere, and when they were in sight of a mountain (Purgatory, as we later find), a whirlwind sank their ship.

Dante makes us feel the power of Ulysses's rhetoric but leaves no doubt that this sole reliance on human resources is presumptuous. This judgment, however, does not cancel the tension between human inclinations and the necessity to restrain them. And this tension is present in the Homeric Odysseus, even though he usually displays self-restraint. Dante cannot have read Homer, and he gives his Ulysses values that are the exact opposite of Odysseus's. Nevertheless, there are enough continuities amid all the differences to suit Odysseus splendidly to Dante's purposes. The *Odyssey* tells us that Odysseus "saw the townlands / and learned the minds of many distant men" (1.3, p. 1), although the poem does not play up the value of this experience for its own sake, as we would expect it to. Ulysses's intellect and its exercise in persuasive speech go back indirectly to Homer but are filtered through the tradition (known to Dante through Latin poets like Virgil and Ovid) of an unprincipled Odysseus. Dante depicts Ulysses's sin as striking at the community, as it involves the corruption of others. By contrast Homer's Odysseus serves the common interest as well as his own (in the *Odyssey* they coincide rather wonderfully). But Dante's emphasis on political corruption surely comes from his experience of contemporary factional strife in northern Italy. Despite the differences, for the first time since Homer we meet in Dante an Odysseus of depth and complexity, gifted with intellect and eloquence. It is a paradox of cultural history that this Odysseus now lands in Hell, which was only visited by his Homeric namesake.

One Renaissance portrayal of Odysseus, in a play whose interpretation is problematic anyway, is enigmatic. Shakespeare's *Troilus and Cressida* stands more in the tradition of the *Iliad* than of the *Odyssey*. Its Ulysses is, on the one hand, a strong spokesman for hierarchical social order, a steadying influence in a world fragmented by selfish betrayal and deceit. On the other hand, his own intrigues, however his motives are construed, implicate him deeply in the gathering momentum of events toward chaos as heroism and love are drained of value as ideals.

In the Renaissance more generally, although the Stoic admiration for Odysseus—conveyed principally through the writings of Plutarch—remained influential, a new reason for devaluing Homer was found. On the basis of the Augustan poet Horace's *Ars Poetica* ("Art of Poetry") and Aristotle's *Poetics*, newly available in the West, rules for writing poetry were formulated, by which Homer was found wanting. From our perspective these rules seem inapplicable to Homer, and the use of Aristotle, who admired Homer, was ironic. Still, the attempt was characteristic of the Renaissance concern with the creative use of ancient culture (Clarke, 106–14).

Also typical of its time, reflecting the progressivism of the Enlightenment, was the "Quarrel between the Ancients and the Moderns" that raged over Homer in seventeenth- and eighteenth-century France (Clarke, 122–35). The "Moderns" found much to criticize in Homer: his gods, who did not act godlike; his heroes, especially Akhilleus in the *Iliad*, who often were not good men; his digressive narrative style, extended similes, and long speeches instead of dialogue; and the manners of Homeric society, including loose sexual morality, the heroes' prodigious eating and drinking, and a lack of nobility (imagine the princess of the Phaiakians doing the laundry. What were servants for?). Critics did, however, have a problem: the magnitude of Homer's poetic reputation. This they met by blaming his poems' faults not on Homer's innate limits but on the primitive time in which he lived, so different from their age with its sense and decorum. Needless to say, partisans of the "Ancients" found arguments for defending Homer. The debate led to a search for the essential meaning of both epics, and the answer that commanded widest assent was that they were intended to teach the politically divided and fractious Greeks the value of order under firm control by portraying the consequences of its opposite: discord and defiance of authority in the case of the *Iliad*, and the king's absence from Ithaka in the case of the *Odyssey* (Clarke, 140–47). This reduction of the epics to political fables would have been comfortably acceptable to Enlightenment sensibilities.

Meanwhile the tradition of allegorical readings, which had

begun in the sixth century B.C., flourished up through the eighteenth century A.D. These interpretations, though at first intended to defend Homer against criticism, could have positive motivations: the assumption either that Homer instructs by delighting us, enfolding an edifying moral within a story, or that he conceals a mystic significance beneath the veil of his text's literal meaning. For the latter approach, characteristic of Neoplatonist and Christian writers, the surface of the text was like the world of the senses, a snare for the uninitiated but a way to ascend to higher truths for those willing to penetrate more deeply (the parallel with biblical exegesis is pronounced). This kind of allegorical reading tended to be discontinuous; it focused on details of the text rather than on the story as a whole. But the *Odyssey* offered scope for sustained moral and Neoplatonist allegory, whereby the hero, assisted by Athena (wisdom) and Hermes (intelligence), makes his way through temptations of the flesh and tempests of the passions to reunion with Penelope (intellectual beauty). The various episodes of his wanderings easily lent themselves to this framework. The Kyklops incident, for example, shows the triumph of intelligence over the low appetites, or of Greek over barbarian. Kirke represents the pleasures of the flesh that threaten to turn men into beasts when indulged in to excess, or, more broadly, physical nature powerless to change the immortal soul blessed with the grace of God (the drug Hermes gives Odysseus). The Sirens can be the temptation of pleasure or the enticement of knowledge undirected to higher purposes (the rotting bones that surround their island bear witness to the consequences).

It is easy to dismiss this kind of reading, but it represents attempts over many centuries to make these remote and difficult poems pertinent to current concerns (which is what all interpretations do, some less consciously than others). And so it helped keep the poems alive. Besides, allegorical interpretation may not be wholly without basis in the *Odyssey*'s text, whatever its excesses in practice (Clarke, 82–98, gives an excellent discussion of allegorical interpretations, which I have summarized here).

Many of these readings, as well as arguments from the French "Quarrel," are mentioned in Alexander Pope's notes to his translation of Homer (1715–26). With this rendering into rhyming heroic couplets, the *Iliad* and the *Odyssey* became first-rate English poems widely accessible to "Greekless" readers. But for a long time from the end of the eighteenth century, Homer ceased to be discussed by poets, philosophers, and cultivated amateurs and became the object of highly specialized philological study. This change is usually dated to the publication in Germany in 1795 of F. A. Wolf's *Prolegomena ad Homerum.*

Since antiquity it had been debated whether the *Iliad* and the *Odyssey* were both by the same poet. Wolf went further: there never had been a Homer. Because writing was unknown when the poems originated (the ninth century B.C., he said), poems as long as the ones we have could not have been composed. Instead there were only separate short ballads. These were arranged in the order of our present texts in sixth-century Athens in such a way that the "joins" between them were still detectable, though the wording continued to vary until the Alexandrian editors established uniform texts. Wolf did not originate all these arguments, but he was the first to put them on a firm scholarly basis. His work had great influence, especially in Germany. His followers in the nineteenth century and beyond, the "analysts," fixing on the narrative's inconsistencies or illogicalities or on allegedly late linguistic features in certain of its passages, evolved highly elaborate theories that typically envisioned a short song on, for example, the Return of Odysseus expanded by the addition of episodes or overlaid by successively longer poems. The first four books of the *Odyssey*, which deal mainly with Telemakhos and postpone the poem's main theme, were thought to have been a separate poem added to our *Odyssey* through the allegedly inept device of the second Olympian scene that begins Book 5. Books 11 and 24 have also been favorite targets of analyst criticism, but scarcely any part of the poem has escaped such scrutiny. More recent analysts have felt able to distinguish the work of two or three different poets, although they disagree on these poets' characteristics and consequently on how to divide up the text. In reaction other scholars ("unitarians") defended the integrity of both poems. At best their arguments were good literary criticism, but they often had to resort to tortuous arguments to explain away genuine problems identified by the analysts.

Milman Parry's work in the 1920s superseded this debate, or at least radically changed its terms. His demonstration of the heav-

23

ily formulaic nature of Homeric language made it increasingly clear that the poems were the product of an oral poetic tradition of great antiquity. The analysts and unitarians had been aware of this possibility but had been unable to free themselves of presuppositions formed by their own familiarity with writing. Parry argued, by contrast, that there are great differences between written and oral texts, in their essential qualities as well as in their origins. Oral composition, for example, especially in such long poems, might account for the contradictions that troubled the analysts and that would not be expected in written texts.

Parry's theories seemed to coincide in some ways with developments in other fields, although the limits of this convergence have since become clear. The results of archaeology, beginning with Heinrich Schliemann's excavations at Troy and Mycenae in the nineteenth century, revealed that the poems contain some genuine reminiscences of Mycenaean material culture that would have been transmitted over centuries through the oral tradition, as well as many more references to objects from later times down to the eighth century B.C. At such Mycenaean sites as Pylos and Mycenae, and at Knossos in Krete where they date from the period of Mycenaean occupation, clay tablets were found inscribed with a script referred to as Linear B. Michael Ventris's decipherment in the early 1950s revealed the language as an early form of Greek and the tablets as palace records and inventories. The result for our understanding of Homer is mixed: on the one hand, the tablets afford considerable knowledge of Mycenaean political and economic organization; on the other, they bring home to us the many differences between Homeric and Mycenaean societies.

Parry's early death prevented him from fully exploring the implications of his findings. That has been the task of much scholarship after him. In particular, his theory has given rise to difficult problems of interpretation. Many have questioned whether orally composed poetry can be approached through our usual methods of literary analysis. If, for example, a given phrase is formulaic, it would appear to be used simply for metrical convenience and not for a calculated poetic effect in its context. Some scholars have therefore tried to understand Homer's epics in different terms as oral texts, often with recourse to comparative material from cultures with living traditions of oral poetry (Parry and, after his death,

24

Albert Lord studied such a tradition in Yugoslavia). In their view the poet may not have much choice or interest in how to deploy individual words and phrases; his artistry would lie in the construction of scenes and their integration into the whole poem. And these scholars have emphasized the adaptation of traditional motifs and narrative patterns into particular contexts. The *Odyssey*, with its archetypal story of absence and return, has proved a rich field for such study.

Others, however, think that such long poems must have been composed in writing rather than orally, although perhaps still according to the habits of oral composition. They can point to evidence for writing in Greece roughly contemporary with the poems' origin. Debate continues to this day over this and related questions: Written or oral composition? Are these alternatives in fact mutually exclusive? Does the mode of composition really matter after all to our reading of these texts as poems? Parry's views have been modified in other ways too, profound though their influence has been. A number of studies of Homeric language and meter have refined Parry's conclusions and in particular have tended to question whether the formular system was as inflexible as Parry thought it; the poet might, then, have had more of a hand in choosing, or creating, phrases than had appeared to be the case.

Meanwhile Homeric archaeology and Mycenaean studies continue. In a different attempt to place the poems in their historical and cultural context, considerable attention has been devoted to the dynamics of Homeric society, often with the aid of concepts and comparative material from anthropology. Here it has been necessary to sort out Mycenaean, Dark Age, and eighth-century elements of that society. Especially of late, scholars have detected in the poems reflections of contemporary social tensions that were to lead to remarkable developments in succeeding centuries.

One historicizing approach has been more popular among general readers of the *Odyssey* than among scholars: the attempt to trace the route of Odysseus's wanderings in the Mediterranean and often in the Atlantic Ocean as well. This speculation was already widespread in antiquity, when Skylla and Kharybdis, for example, were located in the Strait of Messene between Sicily and Italy, and the Kyklops on the southern coast of Sicily. The acid comment of the Alexandrian scholar Eratosthenes says all that is necessary:

"They'll find where Odysseus wandered when they find the leather-worker who stitched together the bag of winds."

So many questions cluster around Homer's epics that for a time their qualities as poems seem often to have been ignored. There have, however, been two significant modern literary responses to the *Odyssey*. Tennyson's poem *Ulysses* (1842) is an inner monologue by Odysseus who, now at home and unable to be content, determines to set sail again "to follow knowledge like a sinking star" with the remnants of his crew (who are imagined, un-Homerically, to have survived). The poem is finely balanced between a recognition of declining powers in old age and a resolve to continue striving out of duty to one's humanity. Dante is obviously one of several strong influences on the poem, but Tennyson takes Ulysses out of Hell and makes him represent not sin but human nature fulfilling itself. In this sense the poem is a fine expression of romanticism. It is also interesting because, like Nikos Kazantsakis's *Odyssey* (1938), it reflects the difficulty many readers have in believing that Odysseus could settle down after his turbulent life abroad, that quiet prosperity is a fitting reward for so much striving. This difficulty may be due to a difference in outlook and values between modern and ancient times or to an inability to appreciate the subtle truth of the *Odyssey's* vision. But it is not a complete break with Homer, because, as we shall see, Odysseus's energy coexists uneasily with his domestic values at times, especially at the end of the poem.

James Joyce's novel *Ulysses*, the other important modern re-creation, follows its Odysseus figure, Leopold Bloom, and its Tele-makhos figure, Stephen Dedalus, through one day in Dublin in 1904, every incident of which is modeled on an episode of the *Odyssey*. The collapsing of time to a single day and of space to an urban landscape, the "stream-of-consciousness" style so alien to the "objective" epic narrative, and the accompanying internalization of experience make this novel a consummate expression of modern sensibility and proof that the *Odyssey* is inexhaustible (for more detailed discussion, see Stanford, 212–22).

Scholarly interpretation of the *Odyssey* has also redressed the balance between the literary and historical approaches, especially in the past 40 years, when it has reflected prevailing literary theory. New Criticism, of which there are some fine specimens among the essays edited by Taylor (see Bibliography), attempted to derive from the poem lessons about life and the human condition. Odysseus's journey and homecoming in particular were seen as a challenge for him to establish his identity. This approach has much in common with earlier allegorizing (Clarke, 102–3), though the meaning extracted reflects interests of the 1950s and 1960s. Structuralist criticism, which stresses the organization of experience and thought in binary oppositions that are then mediated, has found fertile ground in the *Odyssey*, in which the opposition between nature and culture and other themes dear to structuralists, such as eating, loom large. This approach joins literary interpretation and an interest in the nature and workings of Homeric society. There have also been some poststructuralist readings; these have drawn attention to the complexities of narrative, to the self-reflective nature of the text, and to the textual construction of identity and experience that are some of the poem's most fascinating aspects.

Examples of most of the approaches to the *Odyssey* mentioned here will no doubt be found in the chapters that follow. The history of response to the poem is so long that there may seem little new left to say about it. But this survey should have shown that each age reinterprets the *Odyssey* for itself, and that the poem is so comprehensive that new facets appear whenever they are looked for. The *Odyssey*'s challenge to interpretation, to us as human beings, continues. This book, in fact, ends with questions, with which I think interesting new thought might begin.

A Reading

¶

Polis Bay, Ithaka, possibly the site of Odysseus's town.
Photograph by W. G. Thalmann

4

The Hero Absent: Books 1–4

The *Odyssey* begins not with action but with activity suspended. Odysseus is on Kalypso's island "in the sea's middle [literally, navel]" (1.50, p. 3), as far as possible from land. There he weeps and longs for home, impervious to Kalypso's charms and persuasion. On Ithaka his wife and son long for him, not even certain he is alive. Penelope debates remarriage and postpones a decision. Her weaving and unweaving of Laërtes's shroud are emblematic of this "dead time" of waiting. Telemakhos cannot take possession of his inheritance with his mother and her suitors in the house and grows more and more impatient. Yet early on we are assured that the time has come for this period of suspension to end and for events to move forward (1.16–17, p. 2). The process of ending is the poem's subject. It is still accompanied by suspense and delay, which culminate finally in Odysseus's revenge on the suitors and his reunion with his son, wife, and father. This revenge, the triumphant convergence of planning and patience, depends on what Homer calls *hora* and later Greeks *kairos*: "not time but timing, or timeliness."[11] In several ways the right time for action (*hora*) and preparation for it form a major theme of the narrative. We should notice first how the poet works his way into his material and orients his audience to this time of waiting and the dilemmas that need to be resolved.

After an invocation to the Muse characterizing Odysseus and mentioning his role in the sack of Troy, his breadth of experience, his sufferings at sea while attempting to bring himself and his

31

shipmates home, and their destruction for eating Helios's cattle, the poet begins the poem proper with Odysseus on Kalypso's island. He then anticipates Odysseus's trials to come even on Ithaka and stresses Poseidon's implacable wrath against him (1.1–21, pp. 1–2). Now the narrative moves away from Odysseus, whose only function at this point is to wait, in order to introduce the gods. Here we might expect to be given an explanation of the reasons for Odysseus's hardships, and so, in a way, we are—or at least the question is raised of whether a morally coherent explanation is possible. In Poseidon's absence, Zeus, thinking of Aigisthos, says,

> My word, how mortals take the gods to task!
> All their afflictions come from us, we hear.
> And what of their own failings? Greed and folly
> double the suffering in the lot of man.
>
> (1.32–34, p. 2)

This first speech in the *Odyssey*, delivered by the king of the gods, would seem programmatic for the poem. It gives the gods' perspective on mortals, especially their tendency to blame the gods for everything that happens to them (as Telemakhos, later in this first book, will blame Zeus for the Akhaians' difficult homecoming from Troy [1.347–49, p. 12]). Mortals, Zeus claims, are responsible for at least part of their suffering through their own moral folly. It is often said that these lines reflect an ethical concern that represents an advance over the *Iliad*, where the gods are often petty, selfish, and vindictive. How true is this?

Aigisthos was the lover of Klytaimnestra, Agamemnon's wife. Together they killed Agamemnon on his return from Troy and later were themselves killed in revenge by Agamemnon's and Klytaimnestra's son Orestes. The story is not at all irrelevant here. It is mentioned a half-dozen times in the poem for its parallels and contrasts with Odysseus's story. Orestes is held up as an example to Telemakhos, who in the end will help punish the suitors. Odysseus's successful homecoming contrasts with Agamemnon's death, Penelope's faithfulness with Klytaimnestra's adultery. The suitors, then, are equivalent to Aigisthos, and their killing by Odysseus is supposed to seem justified.

So far so good. But Athena counters the example of Aigisthos with that of Odysseus himself, detained by Kalypso. Zeus replies

32

that not he but Poseidon is persecuting Odysseus, and only now (1.68–75, p. 3) do we learn the reason: Odysseus blinded Poseidon's son, the Kyklops Polyphemos. That is, Poseidon's motive is personal anger, not justice (Odysseus has considerable claim to right in blinding the Kyklops), and a large part of his story has no reason beyond one god's fury.

The last sentence of the quotation reads, more literally, "they themselves suffer beyond fate by their own folly." The phrase "beyond fate" seems to allow for an area of human experience that is determined by a person's moral qualities and actions and another realm, fate, that has nothing to do with one's deserts but is simply given arbitrarily, a core of irrationality. Two views of human life—that mortals actively shape their fortunes and that they must passively endure whatever lot is given them—are thus related here to two views of divine justice (Peradotto, 60). The suitors' deaths and Odysseus's persecution by Poseidon correspond respectively to each of these views of justice and human responsibility. And other aspects of the story show the same combination of ethical coherence and irrationality. Poseidon's wrath will account somehow for Odysseus's trials after the Kyklops incident, but why was he blown off course and condemned to his wanderings in the first place? Again, the Greek word that Zeus uses of human folly is the same one the poet has used earlier of the companions' folly in eating the cattle of the Sun and usually implies strong moral condemnation in Homer. And so Odysseus's shipmates deserve their death, and he, by his self-restraint and respect for the god, deserves to be saved. But (even aside from the question of why they are hemmed on the island by contrary winds) the men killed on this account were the crew of Odysseus's own ship. The other ships and their men were lost in the Laistrygonian episode (Book 10), where just punishment of any wrongdoing of theirs is out of the question. Anyway, Helios's wrath is essentially like Poseidon's; its motive is a personal affront, not justice as a principle.[12]

And so two incompatible notions of causality coexist in this poem, just as, in early Greek thought generally, two conceptions of the gods coexisted. On the one hand, the gods were thought to care for justice, punish evildoers (especially those who ignored their mortal limits), and protect the order of the world. On the other hand, they could be imagined as capricious, acting on the most personal motives of hatred or affection. The second makes as much sense as the first, for if these gods are essentially human beings but without human limits, then they can act as they please without having to suffer any consequences—unlike mortals. For example, Demodokos's delightful song of Ares and Aphrodite tells a story of divine adultery. After they are caught in the act and released, Ares and Aphrodite simply speed off to their cult centers, apparently suffering nothing more than momentary embarrassment. But it was human adultery, between Helen and Paris, that caused the Trojan War, the disastrous consequences of which are still being played out in this poem. The importance for the *Odyssey* of this dual conception of the gods is that divine justice and divine caprice, each in a different way, help to define the conditions of the world that mortals must understand and accept. It is within these limits, and even because of them, that the poem creates its vision of the successful and fulfilled human life. How easy to be a god, but how much richer, if more painful, to be mortal.

The result of this first scene is Athene's departure for Ithaka to send Telemakhos in quest of news of his father. A second scene on Olympos at the beginning of Book 5 will lead to the dispatch of Hermes to order Kalypso to let Odysseus go, and therefore to Odysseus's voyage to the Phaiakians. The parallelism suggests that the two journeys should be seen as complementary actions in preparation for Odysseus's return. But Telemakhos's voyage leads to few or no results and might seem just another way of marking time, and Odysseus's predicament is left dangling for four books. Why does the poem's action begin on Ithaka rather than with Kalypso, and why does it then move to Pylos and Sparta? Possible answers have to do with the poem's major themes and its depiction of certain characters, especially Telemakhos.

The first two books give a vivid impression of the state of things on Ithaka in Odysseus's absence. With the suitors' presence—their violation of the norms of hospitality and of wooing (see 18.274–80, p. 345)—civilized order has been overthrown. The substance of the household is being consumed—literally—by the suitors' prodigious eating. The hierarchical structure of the house is weak in the absence of anyone to fill the position at the top. Telemakhos's attempts to assert his authority in the house, though taken seriously by his mother (1.345–64, p. 12), are met with ridicule by the suitors. These opening books, then, show how urgent is the need for Odysseus to return and restore order.

The household, which includes not only the "nuclear family" but also relatives, free workers, and slaves, and not only the house but lands outside the town on which livestock grazes and crops are raised, is the basic unit of Homeric society (Finley, 57–63). It forms a nexus of relationships with other households, both local and foreign, on the basis of reciprocal exchanges (marriages, gifts), and in this way the larger community is constructed. Its order and prosperity depend on the stability of each household, but especially that of the king. And so what is at stake in Odysseus's return is not just his private wealth and standing but also the very existence of a community based on civilized norms. The situation on Ithaka stresses the value of that community and those standards by presenting their opposite.

Pylos and Sparta embody, by contrast, the civilized ideal and show what Ithaka could be if Odysseus, like Nestor and Menelaos, should return from Troy and resume his position. The decorum of life there contrasts with the near-anarchy on Ithaka in two particular respects. The first point of contrast is political order. The morning after Telemakhos's arrival, Nestor leaves his room and sits before the gate on a seat of polished stone, on which his father, Neleus, had sat before him, and gives instructions to his sons to prepare a sacrifice to Athena (3.404–17, p.47). The seat is an emblem of kingship and control and of the orderly succession of authority from father to son. In Telemakhos's case that succession is not at all assured, and on Ithaka Odysseus's absence has left a political void. When in Book 2 Telemakhos calls an assembly to give the suitors public orders to leave his house, the aged Eurynomos comments that no assembly has been held since Odysseus left for Troy (2.25–27, p. 20)—for 20 years. The assembly is a fundamental institution, and convening it is a mark of authority. Evidently in Odysseus's absence there has been no one with the standing or interest to do so. And although Telemakhos, in convening the assembly, is now asserting his authority, the suitors face him and his partisans down.

The second point of contrast is feasting and hospitality. Eating is a prominent concern of the poem—what one eats, under what circumstances, and with whom—because the sharing of food is the consummate expression of civilization. It is a celebration of peace and prosperity, a reaffirmation of communal values, and a way of expressing and cementing relations with others. When Telemakhos comes on them, Nestor and Menelaos are both holding feasts. Nestor is sacrificing to Poseidon; sacrifice, involving as it does the burning of some parts of the victim and the eating of other parts, signifies the relations between mortals and gods. Menelaos is celebrating the marriages of his daughter and son, unions that create relationships on the human plane between households and between communities.

Hospitality involves the sharing of food in ancient as in modern society. The reception of Telemakhos as a guest by the two kings gives rise to detailed scenes of hospitality, for which there is a clear sequence. If a stranger comes to your house, you must take him in and not refuse him. The first thing is to give him a meal, and this act puts you into a special relation with him. After the meal, and only then, you ask his name and home. You maintain him in your house for as long as he wants to stay, and, on the other hand, when he wants to leave you do not keep him against his will. You instead help him on his way. When he departs, you give him a guest gift. The guest-host relation lasts permanently after the visit (you can then visit your former guest in his home) and can even be inherited by the two parties' sons. This relationship, like so much else in Homeric society, is expressed in a tangible object—the guest gift, given by host to guest when the latter departs.

Scenes of feasting and hospitality occur throughout the *Odyssey*; scholars call them type scenes and refer them to the tradition of oral composition that stands behind this poem. But though typical, they are always significant as expressions of civilized behavior, and the scenes at Pylos and Sparta seem in calculated contrast with the situation on Ithaka. The suitors violate the codes that regulate feasting and hospitality by their own conduct in Odysseus's house and because they interfere with Telemakhos's ability to receive other guests. When the disguised Athena visits Telemakhos in Book 1, he can offer her food and speak with her, but only in a corner of the hall. Throughout the scene their conversation has as background the singing and dancing with which the suitors amuse themselves (see 1.144–57, p. 6). Later Telemakhos will feel unable to receive Theoklymenos as his guest and will send him to another house (15.512–20, p. 284).

Besides the state of affairs on Ithaka, we learn much in the first four books about Odysseus through others' recollections of him. Penelope remembers him as a husband, the loyal Ithakans as a king "like a gentle father" (2.229–34, p. 25), and Nestor, Menelaos, and Helen as a warrior of great physical and mental endurance, ready speech, and stratagems (3.120–29, pp. 38–39; 4.104–10, p. 56; 4.240–43, 266–70, pp. 60–61). We learn of his relationships with very different categories of people, and in this way we learn about the man himself. In this society a person is defined not by individual quirks of temperament or personality but by such relationships, for these determine and in turn are determined by social standing and role. Penelope, for instance, is defined by how she fills the roles of wife to Odysseus and mother to Telemakhos, Telemakhos by his position as son of Odysseus. And so it is with Odysseus himself.

Personal relations and social roles, then, are part of the poem's overall depiction of civilized life. Other aspects of such relations are gender and age groups, both vividly depicted for the same purpose. The first of these is discussed in a later chapter. Different age groups—their characteristics and what society expects of them—are important because they ensure the continuity of life from one generation to the next and thus the stability of the family and social institutions. Telemakhos is a beautifully realized portrait of a young man making the transition from childhood to adulthood. He evidently has just begun to show signs of maturity. Sometimes he claims adult responsibilities and privileges; other times he shows all the exasperation of an adolescent at the gap between his desires and reality. With his mother he is impatient and defiant. When in Book 1 she asks Phemios to stop singing of the Akhaians' Returns from Troy, he defends the singer (a typical quarrel between a mother and her teen-age son over the latter's taste in music). Then he tells her,

> But go to your room and see to your own tasks,
> the loom and the spindle, and order your maidservants
> to ply their work. Storytelling will be a concern to men,
> to all men, and most of all to me; for mine is the authority
>   in the house.
>
>   (1.356–59)[13]

Penelope gives way, but of course it is not clear that Telemakhos does have the authority in the house yet.

The natural difficulty of this transitional stage is aggravated by the presence of the suitors, and Telemakhos's frustrations are deepened by their ridicule. His attitude toward the possibility of his mother's remarriage is inconsistent. He wants Odysseus home, but he wants to get on with his own life if his father is not to return, and that means filling Odysseus's position by taking control of house and property. The present stalemate in the house makes such action impossible, and so he sometimes speaks as if he wants Penelope to remarry—anything to resolve the situation, which has grown intolerable for him.

One way out is fantasy. When Athena appears in the doorway in Book 1, Telemakhos is daydreaming:

> What if his great father
> came from the unknown world and drove these men
> like dead leaves through the place, recovering
> honor and lordship in his own domains?
> Then he who dreamed in the crowd gazed out at Athena.
> (1.114–18, p. 5)

This fantasy, as the last line shows, is about to be fulfilled. But it points in the direction opposite to Telemakhos's aspiration to adulthood. It is a fantasy of dependence on his father and protection by him, one all the more poignant because Telemakhos surely cannot remember ever seeing Odysseus, who left for Troy during his son's infancy. Telemakhos's confusions and uncertainties will be resolved, and in the course of the poem he will finish growing up, until he proves himself a worthy partner of his father in the killing of the suitors and thus the heir to his father's warrior prowess. The completion of this process is marked in the final book, when Odysseus's father, Laërtes, cries out in joy, "Ah, what a day for me, dear gods! / to see my son and grandson vie in courage!" (24.514–15, p. 461). Here the men of all three generations of the family—Laërtes, Odysseus, and Telemakhos—are together in armor, prepared to fight the relatives of the suitors. The concern with generational distinctions evident throughout the poem leads up to this moment.

This concern and Telemakhos's incomplete maturity help

explain why Athena sends him to Pylos and Sparta, on a journey that in practical terms is very nearly pointless. She sends him after news of his father, and he does learn from Menelaos that Odysseus is being held on Kalypso's island. But this knowledge has no effect on the development of the poem's plot. Athena has another motive as well, as she tells Zeus: "let him find / news of his dear father where he may / and win his own renown about the world" (1.94–95, p. 4). The Greek word translated by "renown" is *kleos*: "what others hear about you," hence "fame, glory." *Kleos* is the basic value of Homeric society, where ideas of a person's worth are tied to the way others, both contemporaries and future generations, perceive him or her. Fame is thus the goal of all heroic action. By becoming known to his father's companions at Troy, by taking up Odysseus's guest-host relations with them, Telemakhos is initiated into the heroic world and its values.

One of a Homeric hero's talents is eloquent and persuasive speech that testifies to his inner qualities. With Nestor Telemakhos is at first shy, reluctant to speak until Athena prods him ("Athena gave him heart. By her design / his quest for news about his father's wandering / would bring him fame [*kleos* again] in the world's eyes" [3.76–78, p. 37]). In his first speech to Nestor, how ever, he proves his worth and the stock he comes from, for Nestor pays him this compliment: "Well, I must say I marvel at the sight of you: / your manner of speech couldn't be more like his [Odysseus's]; / one would say No; no boy could speak so well" (3.123–25, pp. 38–39). When Nestor pointedly mentions Orestes as a youth who acted heroically in avenging his father, Telemakhos acknowledges that "far and wide the Akhaians / will tell the tale [literally, "will carry the *kleos*"] in song for generations" (3.203–4, p. 41). Telemakhos thus receives a challenge to live up to the heroic ideal he has inherited—a challenge that he will meet in this poem.

In several ways Telemakhos's experience at Menelaos's house resembles Odysseus's experience among the Phaiakians. Tele-makhos marvels at the godlike opulence of Menelaos's house just as Odysseus marvels on first coming to Alkinoos's palace. Both enjoy the same ritual of hospitality. When Menelaos recalls comrades lost in the Trojan War, Odysseus among them, Telemakhos weeps, holding his cloak before his face, as Odysseus twice covers his face to hide his weeping at Demodokos's songs of Troy. In both cases the host notices and the weeping precipitates the guest's identification. Telemakhos's journey is, then, a smaller-scale version of Odysseus's wanderings and, thanks to Athena, one without genuine danger. Telemakhos is unknowingly imitating his father. But there is one enormous difference, which the similarities only stress. Telemakhos travels outward, away from Ithaka; he leaves home just as Odysseus is returning. Telemakhos journeys to gain the *kleos* that Odysseus already has. The contrast between aspiring youth and accomplished maturity could hardly be expressed more powerfully or economically than through these movements in opposite directions.

The gains, then, in beginning on Ithaka and with Telemakhos's visits are these: the situation on Ithaka shows how greatly Odysseus's return is needed and suggests that the return will be significant not only as the reintegration of his family but as the restoration of civilized norms; Pylos and Sparta, with their social and political order and elaborate hospitality, embody those norms and point up the sorry state of Ithaka by contrast; the emphasis on generations and on the characteristics and social roles of each age group, exemplified especially by the depiction of Telemakhos, reinforces the value that the poem puts on life at home in peacetime, signifying as it does the continuity of life over time. This introduction to the poem does one other thing, related to these themes and crucial to the poem: it incorporates other stories of the heroes' return from Troy as a counterpoint to the narrative of Odysseus's return. Evidently these stories were told in other poems in circulation at the time of the *Odyssey*'s composition.

At some time a number of poems were put together with the *Iliad* and the *Odyssey* to form a continuous narrative of the Trojan War, from its origins in the wedding of Peleus and the sea nymph Thetis (parents of Akhilleus) to the death of Odysseus (told in the last poem, the *Telegonia*, which succeeded the *Odyssey*) at the end of the age of heroes. This collection formed part of the Epic Cycle, and the non-Homeric poems in it are often referred to as the cyclic epics. Although we have a few fragments of these poems, our knowledge of them depends mainly on a much later summary of them. We do not know when the Epic Cycle was put together and whether its poems were earlier or later than the Homeric epics. Even if they were later, they must have drawn on much older stories, which would have been recounted in epic poetry contemporary with and even earlier than Homer, precursors of the cyclic epics. We can be reasonably sure, then, that from the first the audience of the *Odyssey* knew a whole mass of other stories; such knowledge seems to be assumed by the text's manner of allusion to them. One group of stories had to do with the homecomings of various Greek heroes from Troy. It composed the subject of the poem that eventually preceded the *Odyssey* in the Epic Cycle, the *Nostoi* (*Returns*). To judge from the summary that we have, the contents of the *Nostoi* were essentially the stories told or alluded to in the recollections of Nestor and Menelaos in the *Odyssey*.[14]

In Book 1 Phemios sings "that bitter song, the Homecoming [*nostos*] of Akhaians— / how by Athena's will they fared from Troy" (1.326–27, p. 11). The emphasis on the Akhaians' sufferings suggests a perspective on the Trojan War very different from a view of it—possible in other heroic epics—as an occasion for winning *kleos*. Here the glorious victory after a 10-year siege is seen from the vantage point of its outcome, the Returns. The victory recoils on the victors, who suffer like the defeated Trojans. Penelope's weeping when she hears Phemios's song suggests that Odysseus's absence, from the audience's perspective his wandering, is to be related to this saga of the Returns. Right at the beginning, then, the *Odyssey* puts its narrative in the context of the Returns, and more generally that of the Trojan War of which they form the last episode, as though to raise the question in our minds: Will Odysseus's return be "bitter" like so many of the others, as it seems at this point to Penelope, or will it be different?

Answers begin to emerge when Telemakhos sees two returned heroes and hears from them about others. In Nestor's account (3.130–200, pp. 39–41) the immediate aftermath of victory at Troy was, ominously, a quarrel in an assembly and the division of the Akhaians into two groups: those who, with Agamemnon, wished to delay at Troy until they had propitiated Athena and those who, led by Menelaos, wanted to go straight home. Odysseus went at first with the second group but at Tenedos, the island just off the coast from Troy, turned back to rejoin Agamemnon; this may be a way of distinguishing him from those who got home safely. Menelaos by contrast caught up with Nestor on the island of Lesbos. Why he had lagged behind is a mystery, but the implication may be that he,

41

like Nestor and those with him, will return safely and survive the war, though, unlike them, after an interval of wandering. If so, he and Odysseus occupy intermediate positions between the survivors of the Returns and those who perished, and their stories, as we shall see, are both parallel and contrasting.

Nestor's own story emphasizes those who survived: Diomedes, Akhilleus's son Neoptolemos, Philoktetes, Idomeneus, and himself. And Nestor's sleek contentment contrasts sharply with Odysseus's continuing wandering and his yearning for home. Nestor embodies the fate Odysseus wants and, as we know from Teiresias's prophecy in Book 11, will get. But there is an important difference. Nestor's Return has been just too easy; there is really very little to say about it, beyond a list of landmarks that he passed (3.176–83, p.40). It could never be a promising subject for narrative—especially the heroic narrative of epic poetry. Nestor's Return brings him no *kleos*. Odysseus's Return is, by contrast, filled with incident. And not only will he too finally survive into a rich and content old age; he also wins *kleos* by overcoming the obstacles to his return, including the suitors.

Nestor also recounts a Return that contrasts with his own, that of Agamemnon (3.253–312, pp. 42–44). The parallel between Orestes and Telemakhos has already been mentioned, but Nestor's story suggests a contrast between Agamemnon's and Odysseus's fortunes. Each returns to find usurpers in his house. But Agamemnon's ignominious murder cancels the glory he won as leader of the victorious expedition against Troy (passages in the two underworld scenes in Books 11 and 24 make this clear), for the Greeks evaluated a person's life from the perspective of its ending ("call no man happy until he is dead"). Odysseus's exploits, particularly his victory over the Aigisthos-like suitors, cap the *kleos* that he won at Troy. Agamemnon went directly and openly to his house and so put himself at the mercy of his wife and her lover. Odysseus uses indirection, delay, and disguise. The contrast shows that finding the right moment for action is crucial.

Nestor tells part of Menelaos's story—how his ship was blown off course on the way home and landed in Krete and then in Egypt, where he gathered considerable wealth (3.278–302, pp. 43–44). Menelaos's complementary narrative to that of Nestor (4.351–586, pp. 63–70) takes up when he was trying to leave Egypt and tells of his encounter with Proteus, who helped him surmount an obstacle to his return. Proteus, he says, told him the fates of other returning heroes: Aias, who brought on his own destruction through his folly and arrogance toward the gods and who is thus a clear foil to Odysseus; Agamemnon, again with obvious contrasts with Odysseus; and Odysseus himself, whose story is put in the context of other Returns. After describing Odysseus's life on Kalypso's island, with an abruptness that seems to draw a parallel, Proteus foretells Menelaos's fate: not death in Argos but an existence of ease in Elysium because he is Helen's husband and Zeus's son-in-law (4.561–69, p. 69).

Menelaos's story has some of the same elements as Odysseus's: winds that blow him off course at Cape Malea, sojourn in a strange land (although Egypt is not off the map of the known world, as the scene of Odysseus's wanderings is), riches amassed, an encounter with divinity (the Proteus episode has much in common with Odysseus's visit to the dead in Book 11). It might seem that he sets the pattern for Odysseus to emulate. He is now home, surrounded by his wealth, and reunited with his wife, who is none other than Helen, the cause of the Trojan War. For both husband and wife Troy might now appear to be in the past, as it cannot be for Odysseus as long as his Return is incomplete, and they might seem to have forged a new life together. These illusions are quickly dispelled, however. Although the wedding that Menelaos is holding celebrates continuity of life, Helen bore only one of his children, Hermione, born before Helen left Menelaos for Paris; Menelaos begot his son on a slave woman, and the boy's name, Megapenthes, is significant (*mega-* means "great," and the *penth-* is obviously related to *penthos*, "grief," especially grief for the dead): "Great-Grief," by his origin and his name, is a continuing reminder of the grief that has marked Menelaos's life. And sure enough, no sooner are his visitors seated at dinner than Menelaos replies to Telemakhos's speculation that this house might be a god's by saying that he does not enjoy the gods' bliss. On the contrary, he is haunted by grief for his lost comrades at Troy, particularly his brother Agamemnon and Odysseus:

As things are, nothing but grief is left me
for those companions. While I sit at home
sometimes hot tears come, and I revel in them,
or stop before the surfeit makes me shiver.
                                        (4.100–103, p. 56)

By his account Menelaos's life is a repetitive round of lamentation, surfeit, and fresh weeping. He cannot enjoy his splendid surroundings. Helen enters and seizes the initiative from her husband in identifying Telemakhos—perhaps a sign of tensions between the couple. Further talk of Odysseus soon has everyone in tears on this festive occasion (4.183–89, p. 58).

Afterward Helen heads off any further tendencies to grief with a drug that she obtained in Egypt:

whoever drank this mixture in the wine bowl
would be incapable of tears that day—
though he should lose mother and father both,
or see, with his own eyes, a son or brother
mauled by weapons of bronze at his own gate.
                                        (4.222–26, p. 59)

The drug is described as "an anodyne" (4.221, p. 59); the Greek word is *nêpenthes*, from the same root as Megapenthes's name (*nê-* is a negative prefix, hence "painless"). "Great grief" or a pharmacological, inhuman insulation from all pain—these seem to be the poles between which life at Sparta alternates.

Helen and Menelaos appear to have patched up their marriage. But consider the stories of Troy they now tell. Helen's story (4.240–64, pp. 60–61), based on an incident told in one of the cyclic epics, is of Odysseus entering Troy disguised as a beggar. She recognized and bathed him, and she did not betray him to the Trojans:

for I had come round, long before,
to dreams of sailing home, and I repented
the mad day Aphrodite
drew me away from my dear fatherland,
forsaking all—child, bridal bed, and husband—
a man without defect in form or mind.
                                        (4.259–64, pp. 60–61)

44

Helen is implicitly claiming that before the war was over she had already repented her adultery and was actively helping the Greek cause. Menelaos tells (4.266–89, p. 61) by contrast of Helen's attempt to trick the Akhaian warriors hidden within the Trojan horse into giving themselves away by imitating their wives' voices; Odysseus restrained them (the story of the Trojan horse was told in the cyclic *Sack of Ilium*, but we do not know whether Helen's action was). And so Menelaos produces a counterexample of Helen's continued treachery and hostility to the Akhaians at the very end of the war. Worse, she is accompanied by Deiphobos, her new Trojan husband after Paris was killed in battle. So much for her yearning for Menelaos. Far from having come to terms with the past, husband and wife continue to argue over it indirectly, through representative stories, each tailoring the narrative to his or her position.[15] And the impression is hard to resist that throughout their lives and afterward in Elysium they will carry out this oblique interminable debate: "I did not!" "You did too!"

At the same time, these stories, even while they recall the basic issue of the Trojan War and expose the deficiencies in Helen's and Menelaos's life together even now, point beyond past and present to the triumph of Odysseus's homecoming. Helen's story looks ahead to Odysseus's presence on Ithaka in a beggar's disguise, when his feet are bathed and he is recognized by the nurse Eurykleia, and Menelaos's story illustrates Odysseus's self-control and specifically anticipates the poignant moment in Book 19 when he sits facing Penelope, still in disguise, impassive while she weeps in longing for her absent husband.[16] Odysseus will enjoy as much wealth as Menelaos, with the added *kleos* of revenge on the suitors, and will be reunited with a wife who is the opposite of the faithless Helen. He and Penelope will not be trapped by the past but will build a genuinely happy life on it. Despite the similarities, then, the example of Menelaos finally shows how much more successful Odysseus and Penelope will be.

Thus in Books 3 and 4 Telemakhos meets two figures out of other poems, the *Iliad* and epics about the Returns among them, and he hears from them about other figures from the Epic Cycle. In these ways the *Odyssey* draws into itself narratives from other texts to measure its story against theirs: the story not only of the longest and most difficult of the Returns but also of the most successful one because of the suppleness, intelligence, and dedication to purpose of its hero and heroine.

5

The Hero in Transition: Books 5–8

The other actors have now been identified and positioned. With Telemakhos staying on at Menelaos's house, the suitors lying in ambush for his return, and Penelope's fears for him allayed by her dream (4.795–841, pp. 76–78), the narrative now focuses on Odysseus himself. His inert years on Kalypso's island are ending. There will now be movement and change—material for narrative. Another scene on Olympos, in which Athena admonishes Zeus, again sets events in motion. Zeus sends Hermes as a messenger to Kalypso, and it is through Hermes's eyes that we observe the place where Odysseus has been marooned.

Our first impression is of its remoteness and isolation, with vast wastes of sea between it and anything else:

> So wand in hand [Hermes] paced into the air,
> shot from Pieria down, down to sea level,
> and veered to skim the swell. A gull patrolling
> between the wave crests of the desolate sea
> will dip to catch a fish, and douse his wings;
> No higher above the whitecaps Hermes flew
> until the distant island lay ahead,
> then rising shoreward from the violet ocean
> he stepped up to the cave.
>
> (5.49–57, pp.82–83)

In greeting him Kalypso comments that he has visited her only rarely. He replies that Zeus made him come even now: "who cares to cross that tract of desolation, / the bitter sea, all mortal towns behind / where gods have beef and honors from mankind?" (5.100–2, p. 84). This place is remote from divine society and human civilization alike, self-contained and self-sufficient. In many respects it is the opposite of culture, as Hermes's reference to sacrifice in the last line quoted shows. Kalypso lives in a cave, unlike the gods on Olympos and, of course, mortals. The island is a place of nature in its lushest form. As Hermes stands outside the cave and admires the scene, it is described in detail (5.59–75, p. 83): trees, the birds in them, grapevines, springs, and meadows, all evidently growing without cultivation. What a powerful contrast with Ithaka, Pylos, and especially Sparta, where it is a humanly constructed house that elicits a visitor's admiration. Even a god would marvel at Kalypso's cave, says the poet, as Hermes now does (5.73–75, p. 83). As a paradise of spontaneous fertility and effortless plenty, it is like Elysium, to which Menelaos will be translated (4.561–69, p. 69), as Proteus's juxtaposed references to these two places suggests. That is, Odysseus is already in the kind of place that Menelaos, by extraordinary good fortune, will someday enjoy (Anderson, 79–82). And he wants to leave it. He declines immortality, the unfulfilled dream of most mortals. Why?

Kalypso too is baffled. She points out the sufferings Odysseus must undergo and asks if her charms can be inferior to Penelope's (5.203–13, p. 87). Odysseus never does answer her directly. He concedes that the mortal Penelope is necessarily less beautiful than Kalypso, undertakes to endure whatever sufferings are in store for him, and says in effect that he wants to go home because he wants to go home (5.214–24, p. 87)—no answer at all. This is not the last time we shall see Odysseus glide past questions when candor would be tactless or dangerous. And the situation is delicate. He is rejecting a mistress who happens to be a goddess with complete control over him (except for Zeus's command). He has already shown that he does not trust her, when she tells him that she must let him leave and he extracts an oath from her not to trick him (5.173–79, p. 86). And so in our first introduction to Odysseus after his weeping for home, we see his *metis* expressed in mistrust of appearances and others' words, and in his own verbal tact. But unfortunately he obscures his thoughts from us as well.

We can only guess at his motives. Perhaps he rejects Kalypso's isolation and the stagnation that immortal ease entails as a condition the gods can enjoy but mortals, because of their different nature, cannot. For them pain and risk are inseparable from achievement, and worthy actions can take place only in community with others and within time (which also implies eventual death). Kalypso's name would have reminded a Greek audience of the verb *kaluptein*, "to cover over, conceal," and the implication is that by staying with her Odysseus would be hidden as far as the rest of the world is concerned. Her cave may thus be an emblem of her concealing nature. As Aristotle wrote centuries later,[17] "man is by nature a political animal [that is, meant to live in organized communities]. And he who . . . is without a state is either a bad man or above humanity" (*Politics* 1, 1253a)—like Kalypso.

Odysseus wants human things. With characteristic prudence he recognizes the difference between gods and mortals and what is appropriate to each, and understands the danger of trying to cross that boundary. There may be a sign that the gods too consider the kind of union Kalypso wants with a mortal inappropriate, when Kalypso, in anger at Zeus's command, mentions to Hermes Orion and Iasion, who slept with goddesses and as a result were killed by other divinities (5.118–28, pp. 84–85).

Some overtones of the scene between Odysseus and Kalypso (5.192–202, pp. 86–87) suggest the full implications of Odysseus's choice. When they enter the cave, Odysseus sits in the chair in which Hermes sat a short time before. But whereas Kalypso had given Hermes ambrosia and nektar, the food and drink of the gods, she sets before Odysseus "victuals and drink of men." She sits opposite Odysseus, and her maids serve her with nektar and ambrosia. The distance between their seats and the distinction in their foods draw the line between mortal and immortal. Odysseus is now invited to cross that line, and when he refuses, the meal becomes in effect a commemoration of his parting from Kalypso.

Greek tradition knew of a time when gods and mortals lived on terms of intimacy, which was sometimes associated with the notion of a "Golden Age." This intimacy was expressed in several ways: common meals (recall that the sharing of food establishes and expresses relationships), sexual relations between gods and mortals, and a life of ease and abundance. Odysseus's life with Kalypso includes all these Golden Age elements. But the separation between gods and mortals also took place at a banquet, when Prometheus tricked Zeus over a portion of meat, an act that established forever after the division of meat in sacrifice (Hesiod, *Theogony*, 535–616). This ritual both replaces common meals by maintaining communication with the gods and signifies mortals' distance from the gods by commemorating that last meal. Zeus withheld fire from mortals, whereupon Prometheus stole it for them and Zeus then afflicted them with Pandora, so that human life was further defined in contrast to divine bliss by its miseries. Odysseus's meal with Kalypso evokes both the earlier state of intimacy with the gods and that last feast at which it ended. Resonating with the history of the entire human race, it thus has implications far beyond the individual case of Odysseus. His choice is an acknowledgment that the Golden Age is over and cannot be recaptured, and its effect is to emphasize the positive valuation this poem puts on ordinary human life.

In the *Odyssey* gods do not often eat with mortals, except in disguise—a way of maintaining separation despite the sharing of food. Athena, for example, eats in disguise with Telemakhos in Book 1 and with Nestor, his family, and Telemakhos in Book 3, giving herself away only as she departs. But the poem also depicts places where Golden Age conditions still exist, outside the world of ordinary human experience; Elysium is an example, as are "the sunburnt races" or Aithiopes at the eastern and western extremes of earth with whom Poseidon dines (1.22–26, p. 2). These, like Kalypso's island, help to define Ithaka and the conditions of life there by opposition.

Kalypso has an affinity with the sea. Her father, Atlas, besides holding up the pillars that keep earth and sky apart, "knows all the deeps / of the blue sea" (1.52–53, p. 3). What she and the sea have in common is the threat of concealing forever from the rest of humanity those with whom they come into contact, though Kalypso does so by making them immortal and the sea in the opposite way, by killing them. That is the danger Odysseus must still survive, as Poseidon, observing him sail from Kalypso's island, sends the storm against him. Tossing on the waves, Odysseus exclaims,

How lucky those Danaans were who perished
on Troy's wide seaboard, serving the Atreidai!
Would God I too had died there—met my end
that time the Trojans made so many casts at me
when I stood by Akhilleus after death.
I should have had a soldier's burial
and praise [*kleos*] from the Akhaians—not this choking
waiting for me at sea, unmarked and lonely.

> (5.306–12, pp. 89–90)

Death at Troy before the eyes of his companions in the midst of accomplishing great deeds would have meant *kleos*, commemorated by an elaborate burial and presumably a conspicuous tomb. Death at sea is solitary, anonymous, inglorious, and therefore unremembered. It is true extinction.

Odysseus survives the storm, and his arrival at Skheria, the Phaiakians' land, is described by this remarkable simile:

What a dear welcome thing life seems to children
whose father, in the extremity, recovers
after some weakening and malignant illness:
his pangs are gone, the gods have delivered him.
So dear and welcome to Odysseus
the sight of land, of woodland, on that morning.

> (5.394–98, p. 92)

The simile expresses Odysseus's emotions, but the terms can also be reversed, for Odysseus himself is a father about to be returned to life from presumptive death, to the joy of those who love him. And so the lines suggest the significance to Odysseus's family also of this emergence from the sea and danger, and they thus unify the separate perspectives of Odysseus and those far off on Ithaka. This moment that guarantees Odysseus's homecoming brings him together with them in anticipation.

But a long process lies ahead before return and reunion. Odysseus reaches shore reduced to the very minimum of humanity: naked, bereft of ships, comrades, and possessions, with none of the trappings of his social position (and therefore his identity), unknown on an unknown shore. The books that follow narrate his transition back from the world of his wanderings to human culture. The Phaiakians themselves—humanly civilized in sharp contrast to

51

Kalypso and the sea yet possessing strong elements of the fabulous—are transitional between these two worlds.[18] If the tree under which Odysseus sleeps during his first night ashore is a graft of domestic and wild olive (5.476–77, pp. 94–95; the meaning of the Greek word translated "wild olive" is not entirely certain), then it is an emblem of Odysseus's transitional state. Anyway, the simile that describes him lying on his bed of leaves suggests both the persistence of life itself and (as fire is a token of civilization) his irreducible identity as a man of culture in this wild setting:

> A man in a distant field, no hearthfires near,
> will hide a fresh brand in his bed of embers
> to keep a spark alive for the next day;
> so in the leaves Odysseus hid himself,
> while over him Athena showered sleep.
>
> (5.488–92, p. 95)

At the seashore near the mouth of a river, a wild place domesticated by its use as a place to wash clothes, Odysseus is on the margin of civilization. He will move from there into the city and to the king's house, and from there into its heart, the hall, a place of safety where he will be taken in as a guest and from which he will be given passage home. But if the Phaiakians' hospitality is a paradigm of civilized conduct, there are also tensions in the situation. Civility does not just happen; it must be achieved. Odysseus's progression in the Phaiakians' eyes from a possibly dangerous stranger to an anonymous suppliant and guest and finally to the Ithakan Odysseus, hero from the Trojan stories that Demodokos sings, must be negotiated with delicate tact on both sides. Odysseus must prove himself worthy of hospitality and escort home by demonstrating his mastery of the codes of civilized behavior, just as the Phaiakians must prove to him the degree of their civility.

Odysseus first reestablishes contact with the human community through Nausikaa, King Alkinoos's daughter. The encounter between the experienced and weary man and the sheltered girl is one of the most delightful episodes in the poem, told with a fine intuition for human feeling and behavior. Nausikaa is the feminine counterpart of Telemakhos. She too is on the threshold of adulthood, and whereas Telemakhos aspires to control of his house and deeds to rival his father's, Nausikaa thinks of marriage. In Greek society marriage was a girl's transition to maturity and the way she must fulfill her role in life. It might be convenient to think of Nausikaa as Penelope many years earlier, and of Penelope as a possible role model (by Greek standards) for Nausikaa. From the beginning of Book 6 marriage is on Nausikaa's mind. Athena plants the idea in the dream urging her to go do the laundry (6.25–35, p. 100), and this motive is obvious to her father from the way she avoids mentioning it when she asks him for a cart (6.57–67, p. 101). And so she is predisposed to view Odysseus in a certain way when she meets him.

As she plays ball with her maids while the clothes dry, Nausikaa is compared to Artemis hunting with her nymphs (6.102–9, p. 102). The comparison is appropriate for a group of female companions in a wild setting but also implies virginity and chastity (these being Artemis's characteristics). When Odysseus emerges from the brush, naked except for the strategic olive bough, filthy and with matted hair from two days and nights in salt water, he breaks in on this inviolate group. He is described with a very different kind of simile:

> so [he] came out rustling, like a mountain lion,
> rain-drenched, wind-buffeted, but in his might at ease,
> with burning eyes—who prowls among the herds
> or flocks, or after game, his hungry belly
> taking him near stout homesteads for his prey.
> Odysseus had this look, in his rough skin
> advancing on the girls with pretty braids.
> (6.127–36, p. 103)

Once again Odysseus seems reduced very near to the level of a beast. Moreover, this simile is of a type that occurs often in the *Iliad* to describe the ferocity of warriors in battle, and so it evokes the violence at Troy in Odysseus's own past. The contrast between these balancing similes thus suggests the sudden collision between two separate areas of experience: male and female, warfare and peaceful domesticity, where girls are described doing the laundry.[19] Accordingly it also conveys the bursting in of the mature male, the warrior and wanderer, on the sheltered and inviolate group of young girls—a confrontation, therefore, between generations and genders.

This moment is fraught with tension. In Greek myth and poetry, when a man and a girl meet alone in the countryside, away from the city with its rules of decorum, the result is all too predictably sexual violence. Nausikaa's companions have good reason to run away. The threat is implicit in the situation, all the more strongly because of Odysseus's nakedness. Both will have to deal with it without talking about it explicitly, because to do so would be to upset the delicate balance of this moment. Odysseus will have to head off any fears Nausikaa may have of him even while he enlists her sympathy and help. Nausikaa will have to be equally careful in what she says and does, even though she is clearly curious about this stranger and attracted to him, because any hint of provocation would put her wrong in the eyes of a society for which female chastity is the most rigid of rules. In a scene extraordinary for its indirection and delicacy of suggestion, Odysseus and Nausikaa together forge a small civilized community in this solitary place.

How does a naked man approach a girl? Odysseus debates whether he should run up to her and clasp her knees in the conventional gesture of supplication. Perhaps because that would be sure to frighten her, he decides instead to stand at a distance and use his most characteristic instrument—words: "Immediately he uttered a honeyed and cunning speech" (6.148, p. 103; too mildly translated by Fitzgerald as "[he] let the soft words fall"). And indeed his speech (6.149–85, pp. 103–4) is a masterpiece of rhetorical cunning.

He begins by wondering whether she is a goddess or a mortal. This is both a compliment and a gesture of prudence, since the countryside is where encounters with divinity often take place in myth, not without risk to mortals. But then he likens Nausikaa to Artemis. Because the narrator has just done the same, the comparison shows Odysseus's accuracy of perception, but it might also be meant to reassure her by implying that he recognizes and accepts her inviolability. If she is a mortal, he continues, blest are her father, mother, and brothers—her closest relations before marriage: "But one man's destiny is more than blest— / he who prevails and takes you as his bride." Odysseus, by looking at Nausikaa, because of her gender and age, guesses what must be uppermost in her mind—with complete accuracy, as we know—and appeals directly to it. He then adds a further compliment by likening her to the famous palm tree on Delos beneath which Leto was supposed to have given birth to Apollo and Artemis. The comparison of youth to trees is fairly common in Greek epic, but here it serves as a device for slipping in other things. Delos would be a distant and exotic place to Nausikaa, though a familiar part of the Greek audience's world. That this stranger has been there, that he then commanded troops and was therefore powerful, and that his is a story of adversity—all these seem designed to arouse Nausikaa's interest in him. He concludes with a famous appreciation of marriage when husband and wife are like-minded, wishing it for her. Behind it we may sense his experience with Penelope, but in context it is part of Odysseus's appeal to Nausikaa's preoccupation. It works with the hints about his past to start her thinking of him as a possible husband.

And sure enough, when Odysseus has bathed and Athena has made him more handsome, Nausikaa says to her maids, "I wish my husband could be fine as he, / and glad to stay forever on Skheria" (6.244–45, p. 106). And she in turn conveys hints to Odysseus when she tells him not to accompany her all the way into town for fear of what the watching sailors might say:

> Plenty are insolent.
> And some seadog might say, after we passed:
> "Who is this handsome stranger trailing Nausikaa?
> Where did she find him? Will he be her husband?
> Or is she being hospitable to some rover
> Come off his ship from lands across the sea—
> there being no lands nearer. A god, maybe?
> a god from heaven, the answer to her prayer,
> descending now—to make her his forever?
> Better, if she's roamed and found herself a husband
> somewhere else: none of her own will suit her,
> though many come to court her, and those the best."
> This is the way they might make light of me.
> (6.276–85, p. 107)

The indirect compliments hint that she finds him attractive ("handsome stranger," "a god, maybe?"), and notice the information about herself ("I am a desirable match, since many find me so," she says in effect; "I can afford to be choosey. So I'm available"). Later in this speech when she tells Odysseus that her house is easy to find because it is a grand one, she lets him know that she is rich and a person of consequence. Yet Nausikaa slyly puts the idea of marriage on the lips of sailors from whom she distances herself and scorns as coarse. She takes responsibility for none of these hints, but they are there for Odysseus to make of them what he will.

Thus Odysseus's skillful speech has stirred a response in Nausikaa. He is not just flirting with her. He has a purpose: to be helped in a land where he is a stranger with nothing and where, for all he knows, the people may be hostile. As always, he tailors his words to the character of his audience; that is the essence of his verbal skill, part of his *metis*. Nausikaa for her part has not over-stepped the limits of female decorum (as her society defines it) in the slightest. Of course Odysseus uses her, but in a harmless way that takes full account of her feelings. Neither has committed to anything. The hinted marriage is one possibility. If things turn out differently, nothing irrevocable has been said, and they can part without bitterness. In the brief, exquisite scene of their leavetaking in Book 8 (457–68, pp. 138–39) Nausikaa again marvels at the sight of Odysseus but addresses him with dignity; we might sense regret at most behind her words. Odysseus pays tribute to her for her help but makes it clear that his real desire is to get home.

Through making contact with Nausikaa, being clothed by her, and finding his way into the town, Odysseus has begun to reenter civilization. He still must be accepted by Alkinoos and Arete, and this happens in the course of the long hospitality scene that spans Books 7 and 8. Until the process of reintegration is completed when he tells his name, he remains a marginal figure. When Alkinoos wonders if the stranger is a god (7.199–207, p. 117), Odysseus first distinguishes himself from the gods by his suffering and then identifies himself as almost the diametric opposite of a god—a beast:

> You will indulge me if I finish dinner—?
> grieved though I am to say it. There's no part
> of man more like a dog than brazen belly,
> crying to be remembered—and it must be—
> when we are mortal weary and sick at heart;
> and that is my condition. Yet my hunger
> drives me to take this food, and think no more
> of my afflictions. Belly must be filled.
> (7.215–21, p. 117)

We recall the ravenous mountain lion in the simile that describes Odysseus emerging from the bushes in Book 6, driven by his belly (6.133, p. 103). If the needs of the belly reduce humanity to its most basic state and distinguish it from the condition of the gods, they also bring it closer to animals. But the distinction is never erased; social institutions maintain it, among them hospitality, which is society's way of accommodating marginal figures, as Odysseus at this moment seems to be.

That Odysseus will be taken in is not a foregone conclusion, however. It is true that the Phaiakians represent such an extreme of refinement as to make them almost godlike. The description of the orchard outside Alkinoos's palace (7.112–32, pp. 114–15)—the counterpart in a civilized setting of the scene outside Kalypso's cave (though the lushness is cultivated, not spontaneous)—contains the Golden Age motif of trees that bear fruit year-round, nourished by the west wind (compare Elysium, 4.567–68, p. 69), and according to Alkinoos the gods customarily feast with the Phaiakians without disguise (7.201–6, p. 117). And yet there are indications that the Phaiakians have another, less genial side. They are related to the Gigantes, who warred on the Olympian gods, and to Poseidon, Odysseus's persecutor (7. 56–63, pp. 112–13). Through him they are related to the Kyklopes and were once their neighbors (6.4–10, p. 99): both a strong contrast and a latent similarity seem implied.

According to the disguised Athena, they do not readily welcome strangers (7.32–33, p. 112). In their agora, the center of their civic and economic life, is a shrine of Poseidon (6.266–67, pp. 106–7)—appropriate to a seafaring people but nevertheless a sinister sign for Odysseus. Outside the city walls, however, is a grove sacred to Athena. Unlike Poseidon's temple, it is evidently not part of the city's life, but Athena is a countervailing presence, and Odysseus takes shelter in her grove and prays to her while he waits for the right time to go into the city. Her aid and his own wit will carry Odysseus through, and Alkinoos and Arete will turn out to be consummate hosts. But the menacing hints in the background add enough suspense to keep this episode from being a routine scene of hospitality. We are not allowed to forget that the Phaiakians are part of the alien world of Odysseus's wanderings, of which there are aspects not easily accounted for by the categories of human thought. Alkinoos mentions the Kyklopes and "savage tribe of

Gigantes" together with the Phaiakians as enjoying close relations with the gods (7.205–6, p. 117).

After Odysseus has been taken in and fed and the other guests have departed, he has a conversation with Alkinoos and Arete that, like his encounter with Nausikaa, demands all his finesse to avoid possible pitfalls. Arete recognizes his clothes and asks, with asperity, "Who are you, and who has given you this clothing? / Did you not say you wandered here by sea?" (7.237–39, p. 118). Odysseus begins his reply,

> Ah, majesty, what labor it would be
> to go through the whole story! All my years
> of misadventures, given by those on high!
> But this you ask about is quickly told.
>
> (7.241–43, p. 118)

And he is off: Kalypso, the shipwreck that drove him to her island and the loss of his men, Kalypso's promise of immortality and his resistance, and then the events of Books 5 and 6 (the raft; the storm, shipwreck, and swimming; the meeting with Nausikaa). He spins such a web of narrative that it is easy not to notice that Arete has been hoodwinked. He tells her about the clothes but never answers her other question, "Who are you?"—the first of several postponements of his telling his name to the Phaiakians. His stories not only distract Arete and Alkinoos but also make him glamorous in their eyes.[20]

If she recognized the clothing, Arete must have guessed that Odysseus got it from Nausikaa. A young girl's meeting with a man in a deserted place must appear suspicious to her parents. Notice how Odysseus gets around the problem:

> I prayed her to assist me,
> and her good sense was perfect; one could hope
> for no behavior like it from the young,
> thoughtless as they most often are. But she
> gave me good provender, and good red wine,
> a river bath, and finally this clothing.
>
> (7.292–97, p. 119)

In heading off natural suspicion Odysseus runs up against the opposite problem: Alkinoos takes him too much at his word. If Nausikaa did her duty so well in helping the suppliant, she should have brought him home with her (7.298–301, p. 119). Now we know the reason Nausikaa gave for not doing so: delicacy about what the sailors might say, which conveyed her own thoughts about marriage. Odysseus can hardly tell her parents about that, and so instead he lies outright: he refused to accompany her out of fear of her parents' jealous anger, natural enough if their daughter appeared with a strange man (7.302–7, p. 120). Notice what he accomplishes with this lie. He impresses the king and queen with *his* delicacy (never mind Nausikaa's), and he gets Alkinoos so eager to deny that he is quick to anger that any lingering unease about his daughter dissipates.

In fact he succeeds too well, for in the next breath Alkinoos offers to marry Odysseus to Nausikaa and make him his son-in-law. Now that the idea has been made explicit, it will be much harder to evade than Nausikaa's hints were. Odysseus cannot afford to risk offending his hosts, for he depends on them for passage home to Ithaka—and here they are proposing that he settle with them instead. On the other hand, Alkinoos goes on to assure Odysseus that if he would rather leave, the Phaiakians will take him home. To keep a guest against his will, after all, violates the code of hospitality, as Menelaos says (15.68–74, pp. 269–70). But Odysseus cannot know that the Phaiakians will turn out to be model hosts, and at this point his position seems awkward. He handles it in just the right way, by ignoring the first part of Alkinoos's speech and responding to the offer of escort home, as though nothing else had been said: "O father Zeus, let all this be fulfilled / as spoken by Alkinoos! Earth of harvests / remember him! Return me to my homeland!" (7.331–33, p. 120). And that is the last we hear of marriage to Nausikaa.

Odysseus's account of Kalypso in his reply to Arete may have prepared Alkinoos for this tacit refusal. In any case the Phaiakians try to detain Odysseus with the same temptation Kalypso used—marriage, but this time to a mortal within a community that sums up the ideal of human civilization (Kalypso's divine immunity from such standards can be seen in the way she, unlike the Phaiakians, does keep her guest against his will). Why does Odysseus want to leave the Phaiakians, or, better (because again he gives no reasons), why does his choice seem right? There is, of course, simply the fact that Phaiakia is not Ithaka and Nausikaa is not Penelope. Nothing is dearer than one's own home, as Odysseus later tells the Phaiakians rather pointedly, though with explicit reference to Kirke and Kalypso (9.28–36, p. 146). No matter how it compares with other places, Ithaka is dear because it is his own, arbitrary though that sounds. In addition, life in Phaiakia, like immortality with Kalypso, would be too easy. The Phaiakians seem too refined and too given to pleasure for Odysseus to be content with them. Alkinoos sums up their excellence, for which he wants them to be renowned, in this way:

> we, too, have our skills, given by Zeus,
> and practiced from our father's time to this—
> not in the boxing ring nor the palestra
> conspicuous, but in racing, land or sea;
> and all our days we set great store by feasting,
> harpers, and the grace of dancing choirs,
> changes of dress, warm baths, and downy beds.
> (8.244–49, p. 132)

What is missing here is any effort or achievement, and in particular any thought of heroic accomplishment. The Phaiakians' pursuits are the opposite of those valued by the Homeric hero. Odysseus can appreciate the peaceful life, but he has also earned heroic *kleos*. This passage in fact comes just after Odysseus has beaten all the Phaiakian youths in the discus throw and thereby proved himself a better athlete than they.

Kalypso and the Phaiakians, then, are the opposite poles between which the ordinary life chosen by Odysseus is located and with reference to which that life is defined in both its virtues and shortcomings. Kalypso is characterized by immortality and isolation from an organized community in the natural surroundings of her cave, the Phaiakians by mortality, a city and its institutions, and culture (houses, sailing). But the Phaiakians take culture to its limit, even to excess, and it is this equal distance from ordinary humanity that finally aligns them with all the other beings Odysseus encounters in his wanderings. Kalypso stands for divine indifference to culture, the Phaiakians for hyperculture. Between them Ithaka—"a rocky isle, but good for a boy's training" (9.27, p.

146)—requires toil as a condition of life but offers possibilities of achievement, which is inseparable from adversity and hardship.

Book 7 ends with everyone going to bed; Books 8–12 cover the next day; Books 9–12 are the story of Odysseus's wanderings that he tells the Phaiakians. Though Book 8 is an extended scene of feasting in honor of the still-anonymous Odysseus and nothing much seems to happen in it, a long process that climaxes in Odysseus's telling his name at the beginning of Book 9 has in fact taken place there.

Book 8 is constructed around three performances of narrative poetry. In the first and third Demodokos sings stories about the Trojan War. Thus the fame of the expedition has reached even this remote spot (the first song's "great fame [kleos] rang under heaven," says the poet [8.74, p. 127]), and by a wonderful touch of irony Odysseus, whose strenuous achievements in the war the songs glorify, sits in the audience, at rest and unknown to his hosts. The effect may be partly to stress how his wanderings have reduced him from what he was, but it surely also shows the gulf between Odysseus and the Phaiakians, who have had no part in this or any other war and who simply take pleasure in the narrative while Odysseus, who has suffered through it all, weeps. Odysseus also has the privilege of hearing himself celebrated in song—a reward for achievement only imagined by all other Homeric heroes. From this point of view his weeping seems paradoxical (we shall come back to it in a later chapter).

When Alkinoos notices his guest weeping at the first performance (8.97–103, p. 128), the time for Odysseus to identify himself seems to have come because a similar moment provoked Telemakhos's recognition by Menelaos in Book 4. But it is postponed. Alkinoos tactfully deflects the emotion of the moment by suggesting athletic contests, now that feasting has come to a pause. The contests, with Euryalos's challenge to Odysseus and Odysseus's angry reaction and impressive feat with the discus, prompt Odysseus to show the Phaiakians another side of himself. In moments he is transformed from helpless suppliant to master of insult (8.166–85, p. 130) and physical skill. In his anger at the challenge to his dignity he is a typical epic war hero, and in his reference to his prowess with the bow at Troy (8.215–22, p. 131) he very nearly gives himself away. In any case he involuntarily tells the Phaiakians something they did not know about him—that he fought at Troy—and this and his unsuspected physical prowess make the question of who he is all the more interesting to them. The episode also fills out our impression of Odysseus by showing a side of him, physical might, that complements his craftiness. Moreover, it further distinguishes him from the Phaiakians, whose talents, as Alkinoos says, are for softer activities than athletic contests. His words are immediately borne out by the contrast between Odysseus's cast of the discus and the nimbleness of the Phaiakians' dancing to Demodokos's next song.

That song is about the adultery between Aphrodite and Ares. The affair's lack of consequence contrasts with the terrible results of Helen's adultery with Paris, and the story delights Odysseus as well as the Phaiakians. It is further set off from the songs about Troy by being sung outside rather than at the feasting inside the hall. It provides a moment of relaxation and escape while mortals for the only time in the *Odyssey* contemplate the doings of the gods rather than vice versa. In its celebration of the victory of intelligence over physical superiority—note that Hephaistos is lame, Ares handsome—the story also recapitulates a main theme of the *Odyssey*. Not only has Odysseus rebuked Euryalos by distinguishing between physical appearance and intelligence just moments earlier,[21] but his own victory by strategem over the suitors to vindicate his status as husband will also follow the pattern set by Hephaistos.

After this song the company returns to the hall, and the scene is set for the revelation of Odysseus's name. Odysseus precipitates that revelation by asking Demodokos to sing about the Trojan horse. The story makes Odysseus weep, and this time Alkinoos does not overlook it. The first song concerned an event (not otherwise known) evidently from near the beginning of the Trojan War, a quarrel between Odysseus and Akhilleus; the story of the Trojan horse (told in the Epic Cycle) is from its end. Together the two songs bracket the war, and once again the *Odyssey* seems to be incorporating into itself narratives from other poetry. A judgment on such war narratives and on the Trojan War itself is implied by Odysseus's weeping, especially by the amazing simile that describes his response to the story of the wooden horse:

And Odysseus
let the bright molten tears run down his cheeks,
weeping the way a wife mourns for her lord
on the lost field where he has gone down fighting
the day of wrath that came upon his children.
At sight of the man panting and dying there,
she slips down to enfold him, crying out;
then feels the spears, prodding her back and shoulders,
and goes bound into slavery and grief.
Piteous weeping wears away her cheeks:
but no more piteous than Odysseus' tears.

                                        (8.521–31, pp. 140–41)

This is the result of war: the killing of the men of the defeated city and the enslavement of women and children. It was the result of the *Trojan* War, which was brought to an end by the trick of the horse narrated in the song Demodokos is singing. This war was an occasion for *kleos*, but it was also destructive, and no glamour can obscure that fact. Yet what is truly surprising about the simile is that it identifies Odysseus—one of the victors in the war who took a prominent part in the ruse of the horse—with one of the victims. And so in Odysseus's weeping we see how the war has recoiled on the victors in the hardships of the returns, and how finally there is no difference, when it comes to suffering, between the victorious man and his female victim. Thus the story of Troy seems diminished from the perspective of 10 years later, and it is again contrasted with the subject of the *Odyssey*, part of which, his wanderings, its hero is about to recount in the next four books.

These performances by Demodokos point up several contradictions revealed by the whole Phaiakian episode. Warfare is a way of winning heroic fame and yet destroys cities, the locus of civilization, and the human relations carried on within them. On the other hand, the Phaiakians embody the peace and civility positively valued by this poem but seem deficient in their lack of heroic achievement. Is there any way of finding an intermediate position, of resolving these contradictions? Is it possible to achieve fame and still preserve civilized values, to enhance and not destroy life? The *Odyssey* seems to raise these questions in a variety of ways. Any answers it gives will emerge only gradually and will be implied by the actions and fate of Odysseus.

6

The Hero Wandering: Books 9–12

The *Odyssey* is the first narrative in surviving Western literature that is told out of order. For four books (9–12) the forward movement of the plot is suspended, while Odysseus tells the Phaiakians his experiences from the time he left Troy to his arrival on the shore of Skheria. These are, of course, his famous wanderings, a wonderful blend of folktale, heroic saga, and sailors' yarns, of magic and realism, a penetration into a world beyond that of daily life and so a broadening of experience through the imagination that is fiction's unique achievement. These stories are so good and so well told that it may seem ungrateful to ask what they are doing in this poem in the first place. And in fact it would be almost enough to say that Homer was too deft an artist to pass up an opportunity to tell a good story. Let us enjoy Odysseus's wanderings as excellent tales first, and always. If we also probe and analyze a little, that is meant to deepen our pleasure, not replace it.

We are so used to the "flashback" as a narrative technique that we may miss the brilliance of its earliest use in our tradition or even be unconscious of its effect. Ithaka in the twentieth year of Odysseus's absence was not the obvious starting point. The poem could have begun just as Odysseus's narrative does, with his departure from Troy and attack on the Kikones, and could have proceeded linearly through the Phaiakian episode and his return to Ithaka to the climax in the killing of the suitors and the reunion with Penelope. The choice to organize the poem as we have it shows something about the *Odyssey*'s treatment of time.

If time is a continuum, we divide it up to make human sense of it and of the things that happen in its course. We distinguish minutes, hours, days, years, and, in the narrative that we call history, ages and periods. The beginnings and ends that we assign to historical periods are always more or less arbitrary. We know, for example, that the Renaissance was different from the Middle Ages, but where do we divide the two periods—especially given that certain aspects of the Middle Ages anticipated the Renaissance? In some ways these divisions of time are a human construct, a domestication of something over which we really have no control, but how would we understand history or the world without them? In the same way, a literary text has to begin and end somewhere; it must select a segment of time in order to make sense of events by relating them to one another within a story. Again, there may be reasons for selecting certain points for beginning and end, but the choice entails leaving out what came before and will come after the events narrated (as well as selecting from everything that happened within the period covered by the story), since it is impossible to narrate everything—unless, of course, ways can be found to sneak the earlier and later events in.

The flashback technique is one such way of overcoming the limits of narrative, and it has the effect of directing attention to the choice of the time limits. In the *Odyssey*'s case this device emphasizes the present time of the main narrative, some 40 days in all, as the critical time, when events of the past reach their culmination and a future is ensured by what happens now. There is an analogy with the highly compressed and selective time span of tragedy, as Aristotle shrewdly recognized when, in discussing the construction of tragic plots, he praised the selectiveness of the *Iliad* and the *Odyssey*, in contrast with the plot structure of the cyclic epics, which together told the whole story of Troy (*Poetics*, Chapter 23, 1459a30–1459b7). Homer, that is, has chosen the dramatically right moment of Odysseus's return and restoration for direct narrative, and not the events leading up to it, which, however exciting, would lack dramatic focus.

Temporal relations in the *Odyssey* are more complex than this, however. Odysseus ends his story with the shipwreck that followed the episode of the Sun's cattle and with his arrival at Kalypso's island. He summarizes the story of Kalypso in a phrase ("she received me, loved me") and then says to Alkinoos:

> But why tell
> the same tale that I told last night in hall
> to you and to your lady? Those adventures
> made a long evening, and I do not hold
> with tiresome repetition of a story.
>
> (12.450–53, p. 225)

Odysseus's account of Kalypso the night before (7.241–97, pp. 118–19) was a shorter version of the events narrated directly to us as Books 5 and 6 of the *Odyssey*. Thus the just-quoted end of Book 12 links up with the beginning of Book 5, and the poem's narrative has moved not in a straight line but in a circle, like a dog chasing its tail. The circle is not quite closed, however, as the Phaiakians themselves and their hospitality to Odysseus (also part of his adventures) would be needed to bring the story back to the poem's present. We mentally supply Kalypso and the Phaiakians at the end of Book 12, and the poem is ready to resume its progress at the beginning of Book 13. The poem has looped back into the past, into memory, and then out again to a point almost but not quite in the present. And so the narrative catches up with itself, as we shall see it doing several more times before the *Odyssey* is over.

Something else has happened as well. Kalypso and the storm of Book 5 really belong with the adventures of Odysseus's story but are told in the poet's third-person narrative style as Odysseus experiences them. Yet because they are again told by Odysseus in Book 7, events turn into matter for narrative as the poem proceeds, move from present to past objects of memory (this too will happen again in the poem). The result is a sense of the passage of time, of time as a continuous process refracted through individual consciousness. What does it mean to speak of the poem's "narrative present," as I have just done, when in fact that present is constantly fading into the past? If the beginning of the poem ends a period of empty time on both Ithaka and Kalypso's island, its progress shows us the opposite: time so full of events that the present is unstable, impossible to grasp except as something between past and future. Only in narrative can they be struck into some kind of stability, though at the sacrifice of their experienced sequence.

Past, present, and future are also not kept entirely distinct; there are leaps from one to the other, and the poem locates different points within each. In Odysseus's narrative of the past there are several leaps ahead in the form of prophecies or other anticipations of the future. In Book 12 Kirke tells Odysseus of the encounters in store for him, ending with the Cattle of the Sun (12.37–141, pp. 210–13). Odysseus then tells the Phaiakians of these incidents as he experienced them: prediction turns into present, lived experience within an account of the past. Kirke's speech ends with a warning of shipwreck if the crew members eat the Sun's cattle, and a further prophecy: "Rough years then lie between / you and your homecoming, alone and old, / the one survivor, all companions lost" (12.140–41, p. 213). These lines predict the specific circumstances under which the Kyklops's curse (a form of prophecy) will be fulfilled (the translation obscures the similarity between the passages, which is clear in the Greek):

> Should destiny
> intend that he shall see his roof again
> among his family in his father land,
> far be that day, and dark the years between.
> Let him lose all companions, and return
> under strange sail to bitter days at home.
>
> (9.532–35, p. 161)

"Return under strange sail"—that will happen to Odysseus the day after he tells this story, and his narrative is part of the process leading up to that event. "Bitter days at home" refers to the obstacles he still must face on Ithaka—in other words, the second half of the poem. They are still in the future from Odysseus's perspective as he sits in Alkinoos's hall.

In Book 11, the visit to the dead, past and future again cross. Odysseus encounters the shades of people out of his own past: Elpenor, his mother, and comrades at Troy. Agamemnon tells of his murder, so that Odysseus narrates as past someone narrating a prior event. But Odysseus also meets Teiresias, who foretells not only the episode of the Cattle of the Sun and the killing of the suitors (past and future, respectively, to Odysseus as he speaks to the Phaiakians) but also the course of events after the conclusion of the *Odyssey*: Odysseus's journey to propitiate Poseidon, his prosperous old age, and finally his death (11. 119–37, pp. 188–89). But in death Odysseus will return to the place where he speaks with Teiresias ("twice mortal" Kirke calls him and his men [12.22, p. 210]). Thus in a movement that balances Odysseus's narrative of the past in Books 9–12, the story moves out into the future, even beyond the end of the poem, and circles back to the land of the dead.[22]

If death is the end of Odysseus's story, as it is the end of every life story, and if the present is always turning into the past or is seen as transitional to the future and is therefore elusive, then we are led to ask what value any human achievements can have. One answer might be that narrative itself, with its power to order and reorder time as the *Odyssey* does, is a way of giving events a kind of stability and permanence beyond the limits of the individual's lifetime. It works through memory to preserve the past, and by bringing past, present, and future into relation with one another it gives perspective on all three. In particular, in the form of epic poetry it preserves past deeds and people in the memory of future generations and of the entire culture. That is why *kleos* is so important to Homeric heroes and why Odysseus despairs so when, in Book 5, it appears that he will perish without a trace in the storm. In his triumph over the suitors and his achievement of a successful life Odysseus will snatch something from the process of time that will be given permanence through poetry, *this* poem. This is not real immortality, and the ordering of time and narrative material and therefore the understanding gained are a human construct, arbitrary and partly illusory. Still, it is all we mortals have.

"Now I say / by hook or crook this peril too shall be / something that we remember," Odysseus tells his crew as they approach Skylla (12.212, p. 216). Books 9–12 show him in this process of remembering. Odysseus recounts his wanderings in the first person, in contrast to the rest of the poem, which is third-person narrative. This is another device whose significance should not be overlooked, particularly because special attention is drawn to it in the "intermezzo" of Book 11, when Odysseus breaks off his account and there is a brief return to third-person narrative before he resumes his story. To say that Odysseus tells his story is itself a fiction, because it really is the epic narrator who tells of Odysseus telling his story. But that very fact emphasizes the process of storytelling. Odysseus's narrative is thus an emblem within the poem of the unfolding of the *Odyssey* itself; Alkinoos likens Odysseus to a poet in the interlude in Book 11 (11.368–69, p. 197). One of the effects is to make us aware of what we normally accept unconsciously when we read or listen to a story: its artificially constructed, fictive nature and also its relation to time and memory. As Odysseus recalls his experiences, the poet of the *Odyssey* constructs in our memory Odysseus acting and telling about it. The point of all this is not just to play a literary game or to make general statements about narrative, although the poet of the *Odyssey* clearly takes pleasure in what he is doing and so should we. The self-conscious emphasis on narrative is also thematically significant; like the poem's temporal structure from which it is actually inseparable, it raises the issues of time, memory, the value of human achievement, and the function of poetry.

Another result of the switch to first-person narrative is that whereas until this point the poet has been rather reticent about Odysseus's thoughts, motives, and feelings, we are now given Odysseus's perspective on his experiences and his reactions to them. The narrative becomes subjective. Odysseus tells us of his delight at his cleverness in tricking Polyphemos with the false name (9.413–14, p.157), his contemplating suicide in despair after his comrades opened Aiolos's bag of winds when their ship was in sight of Ithaka (10.49–52, p. 166), his reasons for withholding Kirke's information about Skylla from his crew (12.223–25, p. 217), and what it was like to watch helplessly as three of his men were plucked off the ship and eaten by the monster:

> She ate them as they shrieked there, in her den,
> in the dire grapple, reaching still for me—
> and deathly pity ran me through
> at that sight—far the worst I ever suffered,
> questing the passes of the strange sea.
>
> (12.256–59, p. 218)

And so we get a much fuller and richer conception of Odysseus as a man—a conception that will be important in the second half of the *Odyssey*, when the poet will also be freer about giving us Odysseus's thoughts and feelings.

One of the hardest questions to answer about this poem is

whether Odysseus learns anything from his wanderings. Does he need to learn anything, if the stories of him at Troy told by Helen and Menelaos in Book 4 show him already possessing the qualities essential to his ultimate success? If not, what about his occasional lapses into folly, as in the Kyklops incident (discussed later) or in his staying with Kirke for a year and needing to be reminded by his companions to leave for home? Did the Greeks have the notion that we hold so dear of a developing character? These questions can be discussed endlessly, but I think it fair to say that the Odysseus who goes through these adventures is not quite the same man as the one who tells the Phaiakians about them. The difference is not very great, but the narrator does have the advantage of hindsight over the wanderer. The first-person style often stresses this difference, as when Odysseus comments on his insistence on staying at the Kyklops's cave to see its inhabitant, despite his men's urging flight: "Ah, how sound that was! Yet I refused. I wished / to see the caveman, what he had to offer— / no pretty sight, it turned out, for my friends" (9.228–30, p. 151). Understanding his mistakes and the reasons for his successes may be necessary preparation for outwitting the suitors on Ithaka. In any case, at such moments Odysseus consciously reflects on his experiences (Segal, 22–25).

The first of these experiences, the raid on the Kikones, contrasts with the others in being the only one set in the known world. Warfare is apparently so characteristic an activity that it can be used to sum up ordinary human life so as to set it against what Odysseus sees on the rest of his journey. Where, after all, did Odysseus spend the previous 10 years? But the attack on the city of the Kikones is told in a flat, summary style: "I stormed that place and killed the men who fought. / Plunder we took, and we enslaved the women, / to make division, equal shares to all" (9.40–42, p. 146). This is a recapitulation of the Trojan War reduced to its essentials as the sack of a city. Stripped of the heroic gestures that for Homer are all that give war what meaning it can have, this raid is merely brutal plunder.[23] And the victory recoils on the victors, just as the Trojan victory did in the disasters of the returns: Odysseus's men ignore his urgings to set sail immediately (like the Akhaians plundering Troy, they are drunk [3.139, p. 39; 9.45, p. 146]), and more Kikones come from a neighboring city to defeat them. As with the comparison late in Book 8 of the weeping

Odysseus to a woman victim of a city's devastation, the Trojan War appears here in a diminished perspective, as though once again the *Odyssey* were incorporating and reducing other kinds of stories in order to define its own values, of peace and civilization, by contrast. There remains, however, the paradox that Odysseus, the hero of those values in this poem, is also a "sacker of cities" at Troy and now here (one of his epithets, in both the *Iliad* and the *Odyssey*, means just that). If the challenge he faces is to win his way to a life of peace on Ithaka, we shall have to see how these two sides of him can be reconciled—if they can.

The opposition between culture and anticulture structures the entire account of Odysseus's wanderings, where the world of ordinary human experience, taken as a whole, stands for human culture. Odysseus encounters beings and places that range from the divine or superhuman through variations on humanity (where the differences are most significant) to utterly inhuman monstrosity. Everywhere the categories of "nature" and "culture" are held up for inspection, manipulated, transformed. Ithaka and the life there come to seem a unique blend of some elements found scattered through various scenes in the wanderings and contrast strongly with others. Human life emerges as obviously superior to animal brutality, deficient in some ways by comparison with immortal ease, but still most appropriate for mortals, with the best chance of providing the framework for the greatest happiness available to them. That happiness is not unmixed, as it is for the gods, but inseparable from toil and suffering; it needs to be achieved.

The early Greeks seem to have conceived the world and life within it by means of a series of polar oppositions, such as nature and culture, gods and beasts. Nothing was complete or could be known in itself without its antithesis, and together the members of an opposition defined what lay between, by revealing the extremes. The Aithiopes, for example, who live at the eastern and western limits of the world and feast with gods, help to define ordinary human life somewhere between (1.22–25, p. 2). This habit of mind can often be seen in the structure of early Greek poetry, where long and short passages are patterned by symmetrically balanced elements that correspond to or contrast with each other. The incidents in Odysseus's wanderings are ordered in this way, so that poetic structure enacts the thematic polarities. If we simply list them in the order in which they occurred (not the order in which they are narrated, which puts the two last incidents, Kalypso and the Phaiakians, first), it will be seen that each pair varies and recombines elements of the major contrast between civilization and its opposite:

1. Kikones
2. Lotos Eaters
3. Kyklopes
4. Aiolos
5. Laistrygonians
6. Kirke

7. VISIT TO THE DEAD

6. Sirens
5. Skylla
4. Cattle of the Sun
3. Kharybdis
2. Kalypso
1. Phaiakians

This list is slightly misleading in one respect: Odysseus returns to Kirke after the visit to the dead, so that her episode enfolds that one. But for the sake of discussion it is best to consider Odysseus's encounter with her as preceding the scene with the dead; that part of her story, after all, brings out her character and the danger and temptation she poses to Odysseus.

The first pairing (1) aligns the Kikones with the Phaiakians, the first episode with the last. Odysseus arrives at the Kikones' city fresh from the Trojan victory, with all his ships and men and with wealth plundered from Troy. And he comes as an aggressor. He arrives on the shore of Skheria naked, stripped of followers and possessions, and as a suppliant. Clothed, fed, and helped on his way by the Phaiakians, he is now not a destroyer of a city but the beneficiary of the civility a city makes possible. When he leaves the Phaiakians, he takes wealth, more than he would have brought home from Troy, but in the form of guest gifts, not plunder.

The Lotos Eaters and Kalypso (2) tempt with forgetfulness of homecoming in a changeless, carefree present. Both offer hospitality in the form of food, and from a human perspective Kalypso's nektar and ambrosia, the food of immortals, do not differ much from the lotos. Immortality is simply a heightened and permanent form of the state that eating the lotos induces. Odysseus's coercion of his three companions who have tasted the lotos back onto the ship corresponds to his self-discipline in remembering home for seven years on Kalypso's island.

The next pair of incidents (3) shows the opposite way of losing one's homecoming: not through eating but through being swallowed. The Kyklops, son of the sea god Poseidon, personifies the sea in an enlarged and distorted human form, and his eating of Odysseus's men, like his cave, represents the sea's power of swallowing people up without a trace. The whirlpool Kharybdis is the sea reduced to its elemental form: a great devouring maw. It is just possible that the fig tree to which Odysseus clings as he hangs above Kharybdis corresponds to the olive-wood stake with which he puts out Polyphemos's eye, for in the poem wood, especially of the olive, tends to be associated with Odysseus's salvation and restoration to home (other examples are the olive-wood haft of the ax Kalypso gives him to build his raft, [5.236, p. 88], the hybrid olive beneath which he sleeps and whose shelter keeps him alive [5.476–77, pp. 94–95], the olive tree that overhangs the cave of the nymphs on Ithaka [13.346, p. 241], and his and Penelope's bed, made from the living trunk of an olive tree [23.190–201, p. 435]).[24] In any case the coming of late afternoon, when Kharybdis regurgitates the mast and keel of Odysseus's ship (wood again), is marked in a way that brilliantly evokes the role Odysseus longs to fulfill in society and contrasts the community and order of a city, on land, with this desolate spot in the formless sea:

> And ah! how long, with what desire, I waited!
> till, at the twilight hour, when one who hears
> and judges pleas in the marketplace all day
> between contentious men, goes home to supper,
> the long poles at last reared from the sea.
>
> (12.439–41, p. 224)

The episodes of Aiolos and the Cattle of the Sun (4) are linked because it is the crew's lack of self-control (curiosity in the one case, appetite in the other) that brings disaster both times. In addition, Aiolos represents decorous feasting (hospitality), whereas in the later episode Odysseus's companions eat the wrong thing in a sacrifice that is marked as flawed by the absence of barley to scatter on the victims and of wine for libations (contrast the proper sacrifice at 3.447–63, p. 48). The Laistrygonians and Skylla (5) are both cannibals. But Skylla is a monster who lives alone in a cave; the Laistrygonians are human in form and live together in a city just like cities in the human world. Finally, Kirke and the Sirens (6) both work by magic, Kirke by charms and spells and the Sirens by the "enchantment" of their singing (the word is used several times in connection with them, as it is elsewhere in early Greek poetry for the effect of song). Kirke also sings at her loom; she lives in a house and reduces her victims to animals. The Sirens sing in an island meadow, and those who linger to hear them die and rot away. Both offer the same kind of temptation—forgetfulness of goal, absorption in present pleasure—Kirke through sex and the Sirens through song. In both cases it is Odysseus specifically who undergoes temptation and his companions who get him through. They row past the Sirens, their ears stopped with beeswax, and only bind Odysseus tighter to the mast when he pleads to be let go, and they remind him to continue his journey after he spends a year with Kirke.

These inverse symmetries, of course, do not exhaust the relationships among various episodes, but they do reveal connections that are less obvious than some others. There are, for instance, clear similarities between Aiolos and the Phaiakians: Odysseus is received with feasting and hospitality each time, tells of his wanderings, and is helped on his way, with a favoring wind in the one case and ships that read their pilots' minds in the other. On both journeys he sleeps. In the first case he wakes to find his ship being blown back away from Ithaka; in the second case he actually arrives there and only thinks erroneously that the crew have taken advantage of his slumber to help themselves to what he is bringing with him (this time it is secure in a chest tied with a special knot, in contrast with the bag of winds). The Aiolos episode is thus an anticipation of the Phaiakian story early in Odysseus's wanderings. It seems that he could have arrived home much sooner and more easily than in the end he does, but that this must not happen. Further obstacles and danger are not just good narrative strategy; they also show that the greater the happiness finally attained, the more difficulty must precede.

There are, moreover, obvious similarities (monstrosity, eating of human beings) between the Kyklops and Skylla, as well as obvious differences. It has also often been pointed out that Kirke and Kalypso are doublets of each other, and that is true in that both are Odysseus's mistresses and are versions of the female—an important concern in the *Odyssey*. But the differences are equally important. Kirke lives in a house, Kalypso in a cave. Kirke, baleful at first, helps Odysseus leave when he tells her that he wants to, and informs him in detail of the dangers in store for him and how to get through them. Kalypso takes in Odysseus freely but keeps him against his will, lets him go only grudgingly, refuses to help him (he must build his own raft, though she furnishes the tools), and mentions further dangers to dissuade Odysseus but does not tell him what they are or advise him how to overcome them. The two nymphs, then, differ according to the degree of their civilization, especially as measured by their hospitality.

The sequence of the episodes also allows complex patterns of similarity and contrast to emerge as one succeeds the other, and again civilization and savagery are the main points of comparison. Odysseus and his men attack the Kikones for booty and are attacked in turn. The Lotos Eaters by contrast offer hospitality in the form of food, but this, despite their evident goodwill, turns out to be a snare. The Kyklops, on the other hand, does not offer food but eats his guests instead (and generally subverts the code of hospitality). Aiolos stands as a contrasting model of civilized hospitality. His house and the objects in it are those of the human world; the Kyklops lives in a cave in an atmosphere of pastoral crudeness, with such objects as milk pails and drying racks for cheese. But Aiolos lives on a drifting island whose sides are steep cliffs. He is utterly isolated; the social integration he enjoys goes no higher than the family, without a wider community in which it can take its place (contrast the Phaiakians, or Ithaka). Accordingly he marries his daughters to his sons, for he cannot arrange marriages with other households to create a web of relationships that integrates the individual house within the larger community. In this respect Aiolos is both like and unlike the Kyklopes. They have a number of families living in proximity in contrast to Aiolos, but these do not come together in community. Instead,

Kyklopes have no muster and no meeting,
no consultation or old tribal ways,
but each one dwells in his own mountain cave
dealing out rough justice to wife and child,
indifferent to what the others do.

(9.112–15, p. 148)

In this limitation of community to the family, Aiolos, for all his and his family's civility, is like the Kyklops.

After Aiolos, the Laistrygonians. These are organized by families but have an assembly place where a king gives justice (10.113, p. 168)—precisely what Aiolos and the Kyklopes lack and what a normal human city has. The scouts sent out by Odysseus first meet the king's daughter fetching water from a spring (a reminiscence of Odysseus meeting Nausikaa in Book 6), and she points out her father's house to them (as the disguised Athena points out Alkinoos's house in Book 7). For a moment it seems as if this episode will be another civilized interlude in the wanderings. But with nightmare suddenness the queen appears "like a mountain crag" (10.113, p. 168); Polyphemos was described in similar terms (9.191–92, p. 150). The king, called from the assembly by his wife, seizes one of Odysseus's men and eats him, and in the subsequent battle the Laistrygonians throw boulders at Odysseus's men as the blinded Kyklops did to Odysseus's ship. The Laistrygonians are in effect Kyklopes incongruously given the trappings of the civilized life Odysseus knows. In them the social organization that the Kyklopes and the civilized Aiolos lack coexists with utter brutality.

Kirke offers similarities and contrasts with all the earlier episodes. Odysseus sees smoke from her hearth fire in the midst of a wilderness, as his men did in the case of the Laistrygonians. Like them and Aiolos but unlike the Kyklopes, Kirke lives in a house; unlike all the rest, however, she lives alone, without even a family, except for her maidservants. Still, that house is a pocket of civilization in the wild setting of the island, even though danger is oddly combined with civility. Like the Lotos Eaters, Kirke hospitably offers food to strangers, but again that food is a trap. The differences are that she uses magic, and deliberately so, whereas the Lotos Eaters mean no harm, and that her drug makes its eater lose not the thought of home but his very human form. As with the Kikones, Odysseus uses force on her as well as Hermes's antidote but does so now in self-defense. Like Aiolos and unlike all the rest so far, Kirke helps Odysseus on his way, though now not in the direction of Ithaka but on a long detour to the earth's boundary, the Stream of Ocean, which the Greeks imagined as a great river encircling the earth, and across it to the dead. Paradoxically this detour proves to be the way home, as the straight journey that Aiolos provided did not.

The visit to the dead is less clearly related to the other episodes. Perhaps the contrast between Odysseus's sensual pleasure with Kirke and his sight of the sensually deprived shades after the dissolution of the flesh underscores the difference between life and death (Segal, 40). But this episode seems to be on a different plane from the rest, and we shall consider it in more detail later. It is also hard to find such a clear web of relations among the episodes that follow as we have among those which precede the visit to the dead. Skylla and the Sirens, however, are both of inhuman shape, and both pose the danger of death without homecoming to those who sail by, but in opposite ways—Skylla by eating them, the Sirens through what is usually associated with feasting and civilized refinement, epic song. The Cattle of the Sun are the exact opposite of Skylla in the danger they threaten: not being eaten but being tempted to eat the wrong thing through hunger. Kharybdis is like Skylla in threatening to swallow; she is in fact sheer gullet, without even Skylla's monstrous shape. Kalypso, the "concealer," with her cave presents the same kind of risk as Kharybdis (and, as we have seen, she is also associated with the sea), yet she threatens not to devour Odysseus but to make him immortal. Alone in her cave on its remote island, Kalypso surpasses the Kyklopes, the Laistrygonians, and the monsters preceding her episode in her degree of civilization but is inferior to Aiolos, Kirke, and the Phaiakians. We have already discussed specific contrasts between the Phaiakians and Kalypso. The Phaiakians differ from the other beings encountered by Odysseus because they are characterized by excessive refinement, not, as the others are, by a partial or complete deficiency in civilization. Every detail—their eating, their houses, their social organization, their behavior to strangers—makes possible comparisons and contrasts with the others. And yet their muted sinister side links them oddly with the most fearful of Odysseus's encounters.

78

A complex system of similarities and contrasts, then, links together all the episodes in Odysseus's wanderings. The text plots these relationships according to the degree of civilization and savagery that Odysseus encounters. It uses such criteria as what each kind of being eats (human flesh, plants such as the lotos, animal meat, or nektar and ambrosia), if meat whether raw, as in the cannibalism of the Kyklops and the Laistrygonians, or cooked, and under what circumstances this eating takes place; type of dwelling; material culture—that is, objects and implements; isolation from others, especially possession or lack of ships (to be discussed shortly); and degree and quality of hospitality to strangers. This is a sophisticated ethnography, and in fact some of these categories are used by anthropologists today to study other cultures. Part of its appeal is certainly its intrinsic interest, the broadening of horizons for Odysseus and the poem's audience beyond the known world, the sense that the way ordinary mortals do things is not the only possible way. But this exploration of a remote world also seems to hold the categories of "nature" and "culture" themselves up to scrutiny. Together the episodes of Odysseus's wanderings define, especially by distance and difference, the Ithaka of human life to which he wants to return.

I doubt that Odysseus needs to learn the value that home holds for him; he seems always to have known it, though he has some lapses on the way (disastrous curiosity to see the Kyklops, lingering with Kirke for an entire year). But the text itself is concerned to define that value, and it does so by exploring what is radically other. This opposition between the two worlds is another example of the Greek habit of polar thinking, but from any perspective it also makes sense that it is difficult to know something abstracted from a context, and that anything is much more vividly grasped by reference to what it is not. In this way the *Odyssey* can be seen as a meditation on the nature of civilization and the need for it as a way of realizing most fully what it is to be human. Small wonder that the Greeks of later ages considered the Homeric epics their most important cultural documents. It is also not surprising that culture, which here means *Greek* culture, is made to seem superior in general to the alternatives explored in the poem; the Greeks, after all, were an intensely ethnocentric people. But there are exceptions. There is never any doubt, for example, that immortality or, short of that, the easy life of the Phaiakians is preferable in most respects to human life, with its hardship and toil. Human culture is seen as a compromise with the world's harsh realities. As a compromise it may have other limitations and drawbacks alongside its virtues. The *Odyssey*'s vision is complex and never smug.

Some of the episodes in Books 9–12 are recounted briefly, in a summary style. Others are told more expansively and in greater detail. Two of the longer episodes—the Kyklops and the visit to the dead—are especially rich and will repay closer attention.

Odysseus begins the Kyklops episode by telling what he, as narrator, now knows but what he, as wanderer, had to find out: that the Kyklopes are arrogant, lawless, and without social organization. Nor do they engage in agricultural work (another sign of culture in Greek thought), but—a detail whose significance will emerge—grain, barley, and wine grapes grow spontaneously (9.106–15, p. 148). In fact despite these miraculous crops, we will later find, the Kyklopes have a pastoral economy that contrasts with the city-based household economy of Ithaka. Immediately after this introduction Odysseus describes the island off the Kyklopes' coast where he first landed (9.116–41). This is an even more unspoiled natural landscape than the Kyklopes' pastoral environment, which is inhabited and controlled by beings resembling humans. We see the island very much through Odysseus's eyes, though we tend to forget this fact because we largely share his presuppositions. The description is not neutral, however; it is constructed by lists of what the island *lacks* or *could have*—that is, through negatives or verbs in the potential mood.[25] Goats flourish on the island because no man comes there to hunt. Also because of the island's inaccessibility, it is unplowed and untilled, for the Kyklopes have no shipwrights and so no ships on which to cross over to it. But the soil is rich and would be good for farming if seafaring people should come there, and the harbor is so sheltered that ships would need no moorings.

Obviously this description, along with the characterization of the Kyklopes, sets up the polarity basic to this episode—between nature and culture. The island shows us nature passive and untouched; the Kyklopes—in part—embody nature in its violent and destructive aspect. The Kyklopes are savages from Odysseus's viewpoint, not only for the reasons he gives but also because they have no interest, apparently, in rich farmland, and no means of getting there. Ships are a mark of culture by Homeric standards (and their lack a mark of its opposite) for three reasons: their manufacture is a craft, they allow contact with peoples in other lands and thus the spread of culture, and they have the economic function of making trade possible, specifically the trade of agricultural produce. But in his way of speaking about the island Odysseus reveals more about himself than he perhaps intends. He clearly itches to get his hands on a plow and domesticate the land, control it and turn it to his own purposes. This desire has both positive and less attractive aspects. On the one hand, we see again that the values of home and civilization guide Odysseus even in this remote spot. On the other hand, if we are attentive to narrative point of view we see that the man of culture cannot contemplate nature and value it on its own terms.

Culture is so cut off from nature that when the two come into contact the only possible response is the urge for mastery and power. Odysseus sounds like nothing so much as a modern land developer. It is, of course, true that Homer's time was an age of colonization by the Greeks, and we may hear in Odysseus's words a reflex of colonists' experiences of plentiful and unspoiled land. And it is only recently that we have become aware of the consequences of the arrogance in human treatment of nature. It is not simply anachronistic, however, to say that Odysseus's description reveals the limits of a perspective on the world that is shaped by culture. The Greeks were aware of the restlessness, the inability to let well enough alone, that was rooted in their own culture. To find that awareness implied in the *Odyssey* is not unexpected. In fact we shall see Odysseus unable to leave things as they are later in this very episode.

When he crosses from the island and comes to the Kyklops's cave, Odysseus does one clever and one foolish thing. He brings with him from his ship the potent Ismarian wine, "for in my bones I knew some towering brute / would be upon us soon—all outward power, / a wild man, ignorant of civility" (9.213–15, p. 151). This is the first hint of the clash between the cleverness of the man of culture and natural brute force that is basic to this episode. Odysseus's foolishness is, of course, to indulge his curiosity to see the giant who lives in the cave he finds, instead of just rustling the

81

kids and lambs and escaping while he can, as his men urge. This joining of contradictions will turn out to be characteristic of the episode, part of its complexity.

At first, however, the issues seem straightforward: Polyphemos is an uncivilized and impious brute overcome by a physically weaker man whose only (but decisive) resource is the craft and cunning his culture gives him. Polyphemos is characterized not only by the judgments Odysseus passes as narrator and by the crudeness of his cave and implements but also by his behavior to strangers, which systematically inverts the norms of hospitality as exemplified by Nestor, Menelaos, and the Phaiakians. To begin with, when he catches sight of the strangers in his cave, Polyphemos immediately asks them who they are. Such crass directness is unparalleled in other hospitality scenes, where these questions wait until after the meal. Odysseus gives what ought to be an effective suppliant speech, with a hint of the strangers' distinction and misfortune in the mention of Troy (9.259–66, p. 152) and an appeal to pity and religious duty:

> Here we stand,
> beholden for your help, or any gifts
> you give—as custom is to honor strangers.
> We would entreat you, great Sir, have a care
> for the gods' courtesy; Zeus will avenge
> the unoffending guest.
>
> (9.266–71, p. 153)

Polyphemos replies by defying Zeus, and there is no doubt where right lies in this episode—we think. But it is all the more ironic that Odysseus will be persecuted by Poseidon for punishing this giant. In fact when the Kyklops attempts to be clever by asking Odysseus where his ship is and Odysseus outdoes him with a timely lie, the triumph of *metis* over force is once again celebrated, but Odysseus in his fiction unwittingly anticipates the reality of Poseidon's wrath: "My ship? / Poseidon lord, who sets the earth a-tremble / broke it up on the rocks at your land's end" (9.283–85, p. 153).

But the irony here is still latent. Polyphemos's transgression of hospitality now reaches a climax. Instead of offering food to his guests, he eats two of them. He bashes their brains out and crunches their bones—the graphic description heightens the inversion of civilized behavior.

The next evening Odysseus, the guest, offers wine to his "host"—it should be the other way around. Then Polyphemos asks his guest's name, this time after his meal—on two more of Odysseus's men. It is only fitting, since all the elements of typical hospitality scenes are being inverted, that Odysseus respond with a false name and one that will be key to his successful deception. Of the other two elements of hospitality scenes, the Kyklops does not help his guests on their way when they want to leave but has blocked the door of his cave to keep them from escaping. He does promise a guest gift all right: he will eat Odysseus last (actually he says, "I will eat nobody last"—as in fact happens).

The ease with which Odysseus gets Polyphemos drunk also marks the Kyklops as uncivilized. Although the earth produces wine grapes for the Kyklopes (9.110–13, 57–58, pp. 148, 155), Polyphemos's drink of choice is evidently milk (9.248–49, p. 152). Wine, however, normally follows the meal at a feast, and drinking it while listening to a singer is part of the feast's decorum (9.5–10, p. 145). Moreover, the Greeks always diluted their wine with a high proportion of water, and this Ismarian wine is so strong that a proportion of 20 measures of water to one of wine would be appropriate (9.209–10, p. 151). To drink wine neat—especially such wine as this—was considered sottish. Polyphemos does not know how to drink, and so he is easy prey for Odysseus.

On the first night, after the Kyklops has eaten men and fallen asleep, Odysseus approaches him:

> My heart beat high now at the chance of action,
> and drawing the sharp sword from my hip I went
> along his flank to stab him where the midriff
> holds the liver. I had touched the spot
> when sudden fear stayed me: if I killed him
> we perished there as well, for we could never
> move his ponderous doorway slab aside.
> So we were left to groan and wait for morning.
> (9.299–306, p. 154)

The choice is clear: in this situation, in the world in which Odysseus wanders that is so different from what he knows, force—the reflex of the heroic warrior that Odysseus is—is out of place and can be self-defeating. We might think ahead to his illusion, despite Kirke's warning, that he can defeat Skylla by force of arms (12.226–33, p. 217). There the attempt is only dangerous and futile; here it would be fatal. Confronted by power so superior to his, Odysseus must rely on his intelligence. That requires deviousness, not a direct assault.

And so Odysseus devises the trick of the stake, the wine, and the false name. All three are manifestations of the *metis* that is inseparable from culture. The wine has been discussed. As for the stake, consider the blinding of Polyphemos itself, the narrative of which I cannot resist quoting in Alexander Pope's splendid eighteenth-century translation. It is in rhyming heroic couplets (the Greek lines do not rhyme) and needs to be read aloud:

> He said: then nodding with the fumes of wine
> Droop'd his huge head, and snoring lay supine.
> His neck obliquely o'er his shoulder hung,
> Press'd with the weight of sleep that tames the strong:
> There belch'd the mingled streams of wine and blood,
> And human flesh, his indigested food.
> Sudden I stir the embers, and inspire
> With animating breath the seeds of fire;
> Each drooping spirit with bold words repair,
> And urge my train the dreadful deed to dare.
> The stake now glow'd beneath the burning bed
> (Green as it was) and sparkled fiery red,
> Then forth the vengeful instrument I bring;
> With beating hearts my fellows form a ring.
> Urged by some present god, they swift let fall
> The pointed torment on his visual ball.
> Myself above them from a rising ground
> Guide the sharp stake, and twirl it round and round.
> As when a shipwright stands his workmen o'er,
> Who ply the wimble, some huge beam to bore;
> Urged on all hands, it nimbly spins about,
> The grain deep-piercing till it scoops it out:
> In his broad eye so whirls the fiery wood;
> From the pierced pupil spouts the boiling blood;
> Singed are his brows; the scorching lids grow black;
> The jelly bubbles, and the fibres crack.
>
> (9.371–90; Fitzgerald's translation is on his p. 156)

The simile of the shipwright is crucial here. It gives the blinding of Polyphemos an almost symbolic significance: here culture, represented by technology, conquers the irrational force of nature. Right after the passage quoted another simile compares the hissing of the eyeball to the noise created when a smith dips iron into cold water in order to temper it. Because handicraft is an aspect of intelligence, thematically the passage indicates the conquest of might by *metis*. It is, furthermore, appropriate that a shipwright is chosen as an example of craft in the first simile, since one of the criteria on which the Kyklopes are distinguished from culture is their lack of ships and shipwrights. Earlier the pole of olive wood from which Odysseus cuts the stake and which is simply lying in the cave is described as equal to a cargo ship's mast in length (9.321–24, p. 154)—another example of narrative perspective, one showing the difference between Odysseus and Polyphemos: Odysseus would use it as a mast, but the Kyklops intends it for a staff to carry when he herds his flocks. The simile of the shipwright also recalls another moment when the activity it describes is literal, not figurative: when Odysseus, using the tools Kalypso supplies, builds his raft to leave her island (5.228–57, p. 88; note especially the comparison there of Odysseus to a shipwright). The process of construction, a sign of *metis* like the navigation Odysseus also performs in Book 5 (Detienne and Vernant, 236), is described in detail, to show the cultural man's tools and technological skills confronting nature, shaping it to his uses. This is the positive, progressive aspect of culture that is revealed when it comes into contact with nature.

The name that Odysseus tells to Polyphemos is, in Greek, *Outis*. Except for voice inflection as indicated by the Greek accent mark and for being one word, it would sound like *ou tis*, "no one" (to preserve the similarity and difference, Fitzgerald renders the name as "Nohbdy," but the similarity is stronger than that suggests). In this inhuman world, it seems, heroic identity not only does not matter but can be dangerous; safety lies only in becoming "no one." Odysseus's concealment in the cave, which recalls Kalypso's cave, may suggest this also. But it might be more precise to say that safety depends on dissimilation, on pretending to be no one when you are really someone, on creating and exploiting a gap between appearance and reality, between inner intelligence and the

outer world. That is the essence of *metis*. And linguistically
Odysseus's identity is *metis* and has the same shifting, fluid quality. When the other Kyklopes, summoned by Polyphemos's cries of
pain, ask who has harmed him, he says Outis has. Taking this to
mean "no one," they reply, "Ah, well, if nobody [*mê tis*] has played
you foul / there in your lonely bed, we are no use in pain / given by
great Zeus" (9.410–11, p. 157). Their word for "nobody" uses for the
negative *mê*, which replaces the *ou* of *ou tis* in conditional clauses.
But *mê tis* sounds suspiciously (except, again, for voice inflection
and being two words) like *mêtis*. In fact, Odysseus continues, "So
saying / they trailed away, and I was filled with laughter / to see
how like a charm the name deceived them" (9.413–14, p. 157). The
last line, more literally, means, "to see how my name and blameless
mêtis deceived them." And so we have a double pun and a double
linguistic transformation, from *Outis* to *ou tis* to *mê tis* to *mêtis*. "No
one" emerges as the embodiment of "Cunning."26

But as Peradotto points out, when Odysseus told the Kyklops
that his name was Outis, he could not have foreseen how it would
be useful. That act of narrative providence belongs instead to the
poet of the *Odyssey*, who has deceived his audience and us his
readers into crediting it to Odysseus. "It is metis at its best: a story
about metis, achieved by metis," observes Peradotto (47). We then
also experience what it is like to be the target of a consummate
metis, and another effect is a merging of hero and poet, further
examples of which we shall see later.

Another trick gets Odysseus and his men out of the cave
beneath the bellies of the sheep. But at this point the issues, which
for a time seemed straightforward, get complex again. As Polyphemos recognizes the ram beneath which Odysseus clings as the
leader of the flock, he addresses it:

> Sweet cousin ram, why lag behind the rest
> in the night cave? You never linger so,
> but graze before them all, and go afar
> to crop sweet grass, and take your stately way
> leading along the streams, until at evening
> you run to be the first one in the fold.
> Why, now, so far behind? Can you be grieving
> over your Master's eye?
>
> (9.447–53, p. 158)

Even though he goes on to threaten the most gory violence to Odysseus, for a moment at least we pity him. Odysseus's attitude toward the ram is utilitarian; he is using it to make his escape and will later sacrifice it to Zeus. Polyphemos imaginatively endows the ram with pity for its master (no matter that he is wrong about why it lags behind). A sense of closeness between Polyphemos and his animals comes through, and that suggests a world of pastoral simplicity and innocence (defined as lack of experience of culture's complexities). This innocence is the obverse of Polyphemos's brutality; both result from distance from civilization. The way crops and grapevines grow for the Kyklopes spontaneously and without toil in fact suggests the Golden Age. Into this enclosed, simple world culture, with its craft and deviousness, intrudes in the person of Odysseus, who permanently injures it. Once again culture, despite its advantages, appears somewhat ambivalent.

Odysseus's behavior at the end of the episode reveals an important ambivalence within him as well. When he and his men are back aboard ship and have almost reached safety, he cannot resist taunting Polyphemos, and his voice allows the Kyklops to throw a boulder in his direction. It overshoots, but the wave it creates washes the boat back to shore. Again the crew members row silently out, and again Odysseus—against the urgings of his men—shouts a taunt:

> Kyklops,
> if ever mortal man inquire
> how you were put to shame and blinded, tell him
> Odysseus, raider of cities, took your eye:
> Laërtes' son, whose home's on Ithaka!
>
> (9.502–5, p. 160)

It is very much in the spirit of epic heroism to boast over a defeated enemy and also to make sure that one's name is known. The desire for *kleos* comes into play here, especially when Odysseus has had to pose as "Nobody." The word Odysseus uses to identify himself, translated "raider of cities" but more precisely "sacker of cities," is used most often in the *Iliad* of Odysseus and Akhilleus, and in the *Odyssey* only of Odysseus. It may have special reference in this poem to his role in devising Troy's destruction through the wooden horse. At any rate it is a heroic epithet par excellence and is very

tive when Odysseus asserts his heroic identity in a world that constantly threatens to break it down.

But the logic of his present situation demands self-concealment, as we have seen. And if the appropriate time for revealing name and identity is a theme of the poem, Odysseus could not have chosen a worse moment than now. Knowledge of his name permits the Kyklops to pray to his father, Poseidon, to punish Odysseus, in effect to curse him (9.528–35, p. 161; commentators on this passage are fond of pointing out that early cultures believe that knowing someone's name gives power over him). From this moment dates Poseidon's wrath against the Akhaian hero. Odysseus's proud "Odysseus, raider / sacker of cities . . . Laërtes' son" is neatly echoed in Polyphemos's curse. Polyphemos earlier triggered a trick against himself by uttering Odysseus's feigned name Outis. Now he deals Odysseus a blow by uttering his real name. And his own name, Polyphemos, means "he of much speech," which is ambiguous. Earlier it may have seemed passive in sense: "much talked or reported about"—the giant cannibal who is a splendid subject for narrative. But now it means "he who speaks much," and speech here clearly has its strongest sense of prophecy or curse (Bergren, 48–49). Polyphemos thus goes from being a victim of a verbal trick to being a controller of language and of Odysseus's future. In this episode he gets, literally, the last word.

The Kyklops story, then, is, on the one hand, a clever and even eloquent demonstration of the superiority of culture and intelligence over brute savagery. But alongside this "progressivist" tendency in the narrative runs a countermovement, one Odysseus does not seem to intend: a recognition of the limits of the narrator's perspective, of the damage he can inflict on a world in which he does not belong, and the possibility of conflict between his two most salient qualities, his *metis* and his martial heroism. This possibility will resurface in other parts of the poem.[27]

The visit to the dead is at the very center of the structure of the wanderings, and it is told at greatest length. Here Odysseus, having experienced large parts of both the known and the unknown worlds, crosses the encircling Stream of Ocean and penetrates the ultimate secret: death, which is unknown even to the Olympian gods. He learns what death means in several senses. In an unforgettable moment imitated twice by Virgil in his *Aeneid* (3.792–94,

6.700–2), Odysseus tries to embrace his mother's shade only to find her slip through his arms. "May we not," he asks her, "in this place of Death, as well, / hold one another, touch with love, and taste / salt tears' relief, the twinge of welling tears?" (11.210–12, p. 191). She replies,

> O my child—alas,
> most sorely tried of men—great Zeus's daughter,
> Persephone, knits no illusion for you.
> All mortals meet this judgment when they die.
> No flesh and bone are here, none bound by sinew,
> since the bright-hearted pyre consumed them down—
> the white bones long exanimate—to ash;
> dreamlike the soul flies, insubstantial.
>
> (11.216–22, p. 192)

This is the physical consequence of death: parted from the body, the soul lives a shadowy existence as a faint copy of its former self that can be revived to speak only temporarily by a taste of blood. At the beginning of Book 24 the dead suitors' shades, escorted to the other world by Hermes, gibber like bats (24.6–9, p. 445). That is what mortals can look forward to. We are given no idea of what existence in this place is like, or even of the place. We cannot tell where it is, except vaguely that it is beyond the Stream of Ocean and that Odysseus stands on its edge. Later versions of this place—Virgil's, for example, and Dante's—will locate it beneath the earth and will work out its geography in ever more precise detail, making it correspond to the moral qualities of the various dead when alive. Homer's land of the dead is eerily disembodied. As the text stands, there is some notion of punishment after death for great crimes in life—though the passage on the great sinners of myth (11.568–600, pp. 204–5) has been suspected (perhaps unjustly) of being a later interpolation—but there is no corresponding thought of reward for virtue.

From this attempt to embrace his mother Odysseus directly experiences something else: the absolute barrier that divides the living from the dead. They may be able to enjoy a few moments of shared sympathy, but true reunion, true intimacy as expressed in this physical gesture, is now impossible. From the other encounters Odysseus can observe how the pattern of a person's life is fixed, once and for all, at the moment of death. Nothing now can be changed, and all the possibilities for development and achievement that life holds out are gone. A life is now viewed as a whole, a finished story, and judged for better or worse from the perspective of its ending. This experience is the only one Odysseus undergoes by explicit command as a condition for getting home, and not by mere chance or geographic necessity (Segal, 40). Why is this one episode indispensable? The answer must be that to understand life most fully, its possibilities and the warmth of its humanity, one must know its opposite, death. We cannot all live and die twice, but the text offers us this experience through Odysseus.

From this perspective the sequence of his encounters with the dead is significant. Odysseus first sees death in its typical aspect and its poignancy, a crowd of shades distinguished only by age and gender and thus by social role:

> Now the souls gathered, stirring out of Erebos,
> brides and young men, and men grown old in pain,
> and tender girls whose hearts were new to grief;
> many were there, too, torn by brazen lanceheads,
> battle-slain, bearing still their bloody gear.
> (11.36–41, p. 186)

Next he sees Elpenor, one of his crew members newly dead, who embodies death in its personal and individual aspect and perhaps serves as a reminder that death is ever present as a possibility and can come when it is least expected (Segal, 41). Odysseus next sees his mother but holds her off from the reviving blood until he has spoken with Teiresias. Now attention moves from the shades, who have only the past and no present or future, to Odysseus himself and his fate. Teiresias's prophecy puts Odysseus's death into the context of this exploration of death in general. Odysseus's life, uniquely, can be viewed from the vantage point of its (prophesied) end, even while it is still developing; by comparison with other fates, the true value of what is in store for him, through his hardships, emerges. His mother's shade gives him the sharpest sense of personal loss entailed by his fate, tells him news of Ithaka in this remotest of all places, and serves as a reminder of the passage of time: the Ithaka to which he will return cannot be the same as it was when he left.

Odysseus next sees a succession of women from heroic saga, the mothers, often by gods, of many of the heroes of Greek tradition. Much of human history as the Greeks conceived it is implied by this catalog, so that Odysseus himself is put in relation to his culture's past by the way the narrative moves from his mother to the mothers of earlier heroes. Then, after the interlude that returns us to Phaiakia and third-person narrative, Odysseus tells of his encounters with shades from the latest generation of heroes, his comrades at Troy. The scope then widens again to a more general and impersonal view of death in the punishment of the great sinners. The final meeting, with the image of Herakles, puts Odysseus's trials on a level with the labors of this archetypal Greek hero.

Aside, then, from enlightenment about death, this episode suggests things about Odysseus's fate and heroic stature that are very much to his advantage. In particular, he is measured against the three heroes of the Trojan War whom he meets. For Agamemnon he has words of pity—and appropriately so, since all the glory of the Trojan expedition, which Agamemnon commanded, has been effaced by the manner of his death. Agamemnon recounts it at length, in yet another version of the story in this poem. This time, however, we hear from Agamemnon himself what it was like to suffer that death—an effect of first-person narrative not exploited to such effect again in literature until Dante's *Divine Comedy*. And the contrast between Agamemnon's fate and Odysseus's survival into old age amid a loyal family, with *kleos* intact, is drawn most sharply here.

Next comes Akhilleus. Here the hero of the *Odyssey* comes face to face with the hero of the *Iliad*; this poem, that is, incorporates the leading figure from another text, again to set in relief the qualities of its own hero. The poetic tradition may have involved, as Gregory Nagy has suggested, a rivalry between Odysseus's claim to preeminence on the basis of his *metis* and Akhilleus's claim on the basis of his physical might.[28] If so, then the generosity with which Akhilleus is treated here is all the more remarkable. Each of these heroes pays tribute to the other's qualities. Akhilleus asks in wonder,

> Son of Laërtes and the gods of old,
> Odysseus, master mariner and soldier,
> old knife, what next? What greater feat remains
> for you to put your mind on, after this?
> How did you find your way down to the dark
> where these dimwitted dead are camped forever,
> the after images of used-up men?

> (11.473–76, p. 200)

Akhilleus asks literally, "What more will you devise?" and uses a verb related to *metis*. It is this quality, and the achievement of coming alive among the dead that it makes possible, that Akhilleus admires in Odysseus.

For his part Odysseus praises Akhilleus's exploits in war and the *kleos* they gained him in life and after death and contrasts these things with his own doom of wandering. Akhilleus's answer is astonishing:

> Let me hear no smooth talk
> of death from you, Odysseus, light of councils.
> Better, I say, to break sod as a farm hand
> for some poor country man, on iron rations,
> than lord it over all the exhausted dead.

> (11.488–91, p. 201)

The whole concept of heroism in war is based on an acceptance of death in exchange for a sort of immortality in the form of *kleos*. Akhilleus, in particular, tells in the *Iliad* (9.410–16) of the choice of fates he has been given: a short life with *kleos* or a long life at home without glory. It says much about death that the hero who died young with *kleos* now prefers life on any terms. But his words also make us reflect that Odysseus, even though his wanderings now seem an affliction, has all the opportunity for further achievement that continued life holds, whereas Akhilleus's life and achievements are now over. In the end Odysseus will gain *kleos* from having wandered and from killing the suitors as well as from his exploits at Troy, and he will have a long and prosperous life at home. Odysseus will get both life and glory; Akhilleus could get only one.

And so the *Odyssey* here claims stature for its story by comparing Odysseus favorably with the greatest of the warriors who fought at Troy. And yet Akhilleus's greatness is given its due.

Akhilleus asks about his son, Neoptolemos, out of a typically heroic concern that the son be worthy of and even surpass the father. We last see him in Book 11 "striding the field of asphodel, / the ghost of our great runner, Akhilleus Aiakides, / glorying in what I told him of his son" (11.538–40, pp. 202–3).

The last encounter is with Aias, son of Telamon. The story, told in one of the cyclic epics, was that after Akhilleus's death his arms were to be awarded to the best warrior after him, and that the choice was between Odysseus and Aias. Odysseus was awarded the arms (accounts differ on how and why), and in fury and shame Aias killed himself. Now Odysseus typically is full of conciliatory words. Aias replies with eloquent silence: "But he gave no reply, and turned away, / following other ghosts toward Erebos" (11.563–64, p. 203). The one thing with which Odysseus, this hero of words, cannot cope is silence; his next lame question seems an attempt to cover his continuing embarrassment ("who knows if in that darkness he might still / have spoken, and I answered?"). But the brief encounter also shows why Odysseus survives and Aias is dead, by contrasting the one's flexibility, readiness to adapt to changing circumstances, with the other's eternal rigidity.

Thus at the center of Odysseus's account of his experience the *Odyssey* defines its concept of heroism, partly through the contrast between life and death, partly with reference to heroes of tradition, and especially by confronting its hero with those from other epic narratives about Troy. Odysseus is a great warrior like them, but he is also characterized by scope of experience, the intelligence that enables him to survive, and an appreciation of home, peace, and the ideals of civilization. At the same time, we have seen that these qualities do not coexist in him with complete ease, that his intelligence can be dangerous as well as life-enhancing, and that the values of his culture can be viewed under certain circumstances with some skepticism. These values, their importance and their ambivalences, must be traced further as they are developed in the rest of the poem.

7

The Hero Returned: Books 13–24

When Odysseus, in disguise as a beggar, at long last stands before his house, he pauses to gaze at it as he did outside Alkinoos's palace. Now he sees not a divinely opulent structure but a fine example of a human house. This is unmistakably Odysseus's house, he says to his companion, the swineherd Eumaios:

> See how one chamber grows out of another;
> see how the court is tight with wall and coping;
> no man at arms could break this gateway down!
> Your banqueting young lords are here in force,
> I gather, from the fumes of mutton roasting
> and strum of harping—harping, which the gods
> appoint sweet friend of feasts!
>
> (17.266–71, p. 318)

This house is the center of Odysseus's identity, and its quality expresses his character as a hero of domestic values. His arrival after a 20-year absence ought to be one of the climaxes of the poem, and yet the emotions of the moment are handled with an indirectness typical of this text and its hero. His love for this house and all it means to him—family, possessions, social identity—can be heard as he dwells affectionately on its architecture, but these feelings are channeled into words equally suited to a diplomatic beggar. Odysseus, that is, expresses his emotions but does so in such a way as to maintain his disguise before Eumaios.

The house is not well regulated now. To the order of its architecture Odysseus juxtaposes the suitors' feasting, and again strong feeling—now anger—seems to lurk behind his words. Their presence makes him an alien in his own house. Hence the need for his disguise, and also the fact that his first encounter at his own house is not with a central character in the story but with a figure, like himself, worthy of respect but now treated as marginal: the dog Argos. Unlike the human actors in the story, Argos recognizes Odysseus despite his disguise, feebly raises his head and tries to wag his tail, and dies after seeing his master home at last. He is a figure of continued loyalty to Odysseus and is a foil to those human beings who have betrayed him. Argos also signifies the passage of time, and the time lost from Odysseus's life on Ithaka through his absence; Odysseus trained Argos as a puppy but sailed for Troy before he could use him to hunt and so could not enjoy him in his prime. Cast out on a dung heap by careless servants, Argos is evidence of the disruption in the house. Once again Odysseus responds on two levels simultaneously. He questions Eumaios about the dog with studied casualness but wipes away a surreptitious tear.

This brief, eloquent episode presents the themes associated with Odysseus's homecoming—disguise, indirection, loyalty of the weak, lapse of time—and the challenges he faces. That homecoming—not just his physical arrival on Ithaka but his reintegration into house and society—occupies the whole second half of the poem. It is a long and careful process. In Books 13–16 Odysseus and Telemakhos both return to Ithaka and are reunited; their separate strands of the plot converge. The action centers on Eumaios's hut. Thus, as with the Phaiakians, the narrative begins on the margins of society and works toward its center, with the quality of that society revealed on the way. In this case the rustic hospitality the beggar Odysseus receives from Eumaios contrasts ironically with the aristocratic suitors' treatment of him. In Books 17–20 Odysseus is at his house in disguise. Books 21–24 contain the revelation of his identity, his revenge on the suitors, his reunion with Penelope and Laërtes, and a resolution of sorts.

The narrative pace is leisurely, the climax delayed. But we know that Odysseus and those loyal to him, though ostensibly weak, will triumph; among other things a series of signs and omens keeps us reassured about that. And so we can enjoy the way this plot is worked out, the clever ways in which Odysseus keeps up his disguise, the occasional suspense when it seems as though he will be recognized too soon, and the situational ironies arising from the disparity between the suitors' arrogant overconfidence and their true position. In short, we enjoy *metis* in operation. All Odysseus's previous trials seem to have prepared for this supreme confrontation between *metis* and physical force, not in the larger world but here at home, when Odysseus and three adherents overcome the much more numerous suitors. Like Odysseus, then, we wait for metis to pave the way for action; we await the opportune moment, or *hora*.

What determines that moment? Pragmatically Odysseus has to gain allies and watch for a chance to get the suitors at a disadvantage. But the time has to be emotionally right also. The process of recognition and reunion cannot be straightforward. Before a recognition both parties must reawaken their feelings for each other, their memories of the past, and their grief at separation. When, as is usual in the *Odyssey*, one person knows who the other is but is not known in turn, he or she tests the other's affections and loyalty. When concealment is dropped, the other person typically guards against deception and eventual disappointment by being skeptical that the stranger is who he or she claims to be, and must be convinced with tokens, which become symbols of the person's essential nature. The steps in this process are not only emotionally necessary; through them the resumption of relationships that recognition brings becomes the occasion for the affirmation of identity.[29]

For the most part Odysseus controls the timing and circumstances of recognitions because of his disguise—but not always. One exception is the first recognition in this half of the poem, when he wakes up on the shore of Ithaka and does not know the place because Athena has poured a mist around him. He exclaims,

> What am I in for now?
> Whose country have I come to this time? Rough
> savages and outlaws, are they, or
> godfearing people, friendly to castaways?
> (13.200–2, p. 236)

echoing his words on waking in Phaiakia (6.119–21, p. 102).

97

Athena comes to him disguised as a shepherd boy of royal appearance (shades of Nausikaa), and Odysseus supplicates her, as in
Book 6. Here as well as in Phaiakia, Odysseus will progress from an
outcast on the shore to an unknown suppliant in the royal house to
full recognition. This meeting resembles other encounters too: with
Athena in Book 7, with Hermes and the Laistrygonian princess in
Book 10, and between Menelaos and Eidothea in Book 4 (Fenik,
30–36).

When Athena casually lets Odysseus know that he is on
Ithaka, the scene changes from yet another of his wanderings to a
recognition of home. But Odysseus, always wary, does not let his
joy show. On the spot he invents a false identity and story, and
tries to deceive her. Athena, of course, is not deceived, as she controls this scene. But Odysseus's exercise of *metis* has awakened a
response in her and prompts her to reveal herself. She changes to a
beautiful woman, strokes Odysseus almost seductively—very
unusual behavior for the warrior goddess—speaks admiringly to
him, and then tells her name:

> Whoever gets around you must be sharp
> and guileful as a snake; even a god
> might bow to you in ways of dissimulation.
> You! You chameleon!
> Bottomless bag of tricks! Here in your own country
> would you not give your stratagems a rest
> or stop spellbinding for an instant?
> You play a part as if it were your own tough skin.
> No more of this, though. Two of a kind we are,
> contrivers, both. Of all men now alive
> you are the best in plots and story telling.
> My own fame is for wisdom [*metis*] among the gods—
> deceptions too.
>
> Would even you have guessed
> that I am Pallas Athena, daughter of Zeus?
>
> (13.291–300, p. 239)

What they have in common is *metis*, here specified as a talent
for lies and deceptions with an eye for opportunity. This is what
draws Athena's favor to Odysseus. But this delightful speech of
frankness between two rogues also has its subtlety: it is Athena's

reminder that she is superior to the cunning Odysseus, as demonstrated just now by her deceptive disguise. Odysseus has to concede the point ("can mortal man be sure of you on sight, / even a sage, O mistress of disguises?" [13.312–13, p. 240]), for it would be extremely dangerous for a mortal to boast superiority to a god.[30] But then he slyly says that he never saw Athena after leaving Troy, "not till you gave me comfort / in the rich hinterland of the Phaiakians / and were yourself my guide into the city" (13.322–23, p. 240). Athena did come to him then, but she was in disguise as a little girl ("the awesome one in pigtails"). Only now do she and we find that he recognized her. The gap in cunning between this mortal and the goddess narrows as Odysseus both humbles himself and implicitly boasts. Deviousness is such a reflex with both, it seems, that complete candor between them cannot be expected, even now. This conversation, by demonstrating the generous limits on Odysseus's cleverness, makes a splendid introduction to his assumption of disguise, by which he approaches home indirectly and avoids the fate of Agamemnon (13.383–85, p. 242).

Athena now permits Odysseus's recognition of Ithaka by dispelling the mist and showing him—as a token—the Cave of the Nymphs. This recognition raises questions, however. The landscape, described in more detail when Odysseus landed (13.96–112, pp. 232–33), has some oddly familiar features. The long headlands forming a bay in which ships can ride unmoored recalls both the island off the Kyklopes' land and the Laistrygonians' harbor. The olive tree at the bay's head evokes the tree under which Odysseus slept at the end of Book 5. And the Cave of the Nymphs with its springs—which should be a distinctive feature of Ithaka—has parallels with a similar cave and springs on the island near the Kyklopes and with a cave in which nymphs have seats on the island of the Sun. Unless—or even if—these shared features are formulaic components in conventional landscape descriptions, they seem significant. As the places to which Odysseus wanders combine and recombine certain recurrent elements, so does Ithaka. His island is those other places, and yet none of them in its peculiar combination. It is, for instance, the island near the Kyklopes with its potential for development by human culture realized. But finally the answer to the question of what makes Ithaka unique should probably be that it is his home, and that aspect is to a large extent accidental (though sufficient in this poem). The similarities between the other places and Ithaka and between this scene of divine encounter and other episodes leave us wondering how firm the line is between fantasy and reality, how to distinguish the counterfeit from the real—a point we shall return to.

The similarities also relate Ithaka to Odysseus's wanderings as the scene of his final and culminating labor. His disguise helps him insinuate himself unknown into his house, of course, but that the disguise takes the form of likeness to a beggar enables Odysseus to see, and the poet to depict, the disordered state of Ithaka, from the lowest class of slaves, swineherds, and shepherds on up. Some, it emerges, have been corrupted by the suitors' dissolute behavior; others have clung to ethical and cultural standards but are impotent against the prevailing anarchy. Odysseus's task, then, is not just personal and familial; he must reconstitute Ithakan society. To further that task the disguise allows him to engage in a process inseparable from scenes of recognition: to test the various people he encounters, test not only their loyalty to the absent king but also their treatment of strangers.

It should be evident by now that in this poem the test of any society is how it treats guests and suppliants such as beggars—especially the latter. Beggars are marginal to civilization. They represent humanity on its very lowest level, when it risks turning into something other than human. Eumaios, himself a slave, replies when the suitors' ringleader Antinoos asks him in irritation why he has brought the beggar among them,

> who would call in a foreigner [xenos, "stranger or guest"]?—
>   unless
> an artisan, with skill to serve the realm,
> a healer, or a prophet, or a builder,
> or one whose harp and song might give us joy.
> All these are sought for on the endless earth,
> but when have beggars come by invitation?
> who puts a field mouse in his granary?
>   (17.382–87, p. 323)

A beggar serves no social purpose. He needs, but cannot reciprocate. He does, however, give the society a way of demonstrating its humaneness by preserving the beggar's humanity, bringing him from the margin to the center, satisfying the needs of the belly that drive him. *Food*, again, is the critical term; the suitors' denial or only grudging gift of food to the beggar goes along with their gluttony.

But the obligation to take in beggars and other strangers is not just social but also religious, as can be seen in Odysseus's appeal to Polyphemos for hospitality in the name of Zeus Xenios, protector of guests. This aspect of hospitality as a religious duty is emphasized especially in the second half of the poem in order to make the suitors seem to deserve their punishment as strongly as possible. Odysseus speaks about this subject several times and suggests why the gods should take an interest, most notably in his famous speech to Amphinomos:

> Of mortal creatures, all that breathe and move,
> earth bears none frailer than mankind. What man
> believes in woe to come, so long as valor
> and tough knees are supplied him by the gods?
> But when the gods in bliss bring miseries on,
> then willy-nilly, blindly he endures.
> Our minds are as the days are, dark or bright,
> blown over by the father of gods and men.
> So I, too, in my time thought to be happy;
> but far and rash I ventured, counting on
> my own right arm, my father, and my kin;
> behold me now.
>
> No man should flout the law,
> but keep in peace what gifts the gods may give.
> (18.130–42, p. 340)

Human fortunes are unstable, the gods' gifts arbitrary and unpredictable. The prosperous man must help the beggar because he may well find himself in the same need someday. And so the gods create both dangerous conditions in human life and the mechanism, hospitality, that keeps life from becoming intolerable. That is why, as Odysseus suggests in another passage (17.475, p. 326), beggars have their avenging furies.

The suitors' abuse of hospitality begins with their behavior as guests themselves in someone else's house. Odysseus's disguise is calculated to get them to express their attitude concretely in action toward him. Three times—in Books 17, 18, and 20—suitors throw things at him. On the third occasion Ktesippos, as he throws a cow's hoof, calls it a *xeinion*, or "guest gift" (20.296, p. 384; Fitzgerald translates it as "contribution"). This perversion of the ritual of hospitality recalls the Kyklops's "guest gift" to Outis: to eat him last. The suitors' eating comes very close to the Kyklops's cannibalism. As Telemakhos frequently complains, they are eating the house—eating its wealth or substance, as we would say. And because the house in this poem represents the essence of the person, the suitors' consumption of it is cannibalism that is a bit more than metaphorical. They represent the savagery in the world of Odysseus's wanderings transposed to human civilization. His killing them ejects that savagery from society, and from this point of view has considerable claim to justice.

But, of course, that the issues appear in this way is in large part an achievement of Odysseus's *metis*, expressed in this part of the poem as his cleverness at disguise and role-playing. His performance as beggar is masterly. Not only can he appreciate and talk eloquently about a beggar's moral claims, and not only does he have the patter about the belly down perfectly; he also effortlessly invents exciting and moving fictions about his past, his fall from prosperity to adversity. Odysseus tells three main narratives, to the disguised Athena (13.256–86, pp. 238–39), to Eumaios (14.192–359, pp. 253–58), and to Penelope (19.172–202, 262–307, pp. 358–60, 361–63). (Two others are less important for our purposes: his tale of Troy to Eumaios to plead for a cloak, which also pays tribute to his own *metis* and verbal trickery [14.457–506, pp. 261–63], and his story to Antinoos [17.415–44, pp. 324–25], a condensation of the one he tells Eumaios.) As we read these tales, we can enjoy their skill, and we can discern something of the process of Odysseus's invention, for we, unlike those who hear them, know the sources of Odysseus's narrative material.

First, Odysseus shapes each story to listener and circumstance. His narrative to Athena is brief, with no information about his birth or background, except that he comes from Krete: he needs to explain why he is alone on the shore with the Phaiakians' rich gifts and to enlist Athena's sympathy and aid. He is also vulnerable to plunder; his tale of killing the man in Krete who wanted to take away his Trojan booty may be meant to warn the putative shepherd boy not to make a similar attempt against his possessions.[31] With Eumaios he is expansive, taking advantage of leisure, indulging the swineherd's pleasure in storytelling, and filling out his narrative with circumstantial detail to lend it plausibility. The story to Penelope is tailored to convince her that he actually saw Odysseus 20 years before, in order to rearouse her husband's image in her mind and to make believable his claim to know firsthand that Odysseus soon will return. To Athena and Eumaios he presents himself as an outcast, an exiled murderer and a buccaneer respectively, to awaken sympathy and, in Eumaios's case, fellow feeling. For the queen's benefit he becomes a member of her class—a Kretan prince, son of Deukalion and brother of a major hero of the Trojan expedition, Idomeneus. The heroic world has no more distinguished pedigree.

Second, each of these stories is a pastiche of events from Odysseus's experiences (joined by some outright lies, such as his Kretan origin). Each of these elements is true in itself, but in their new combination, together with some modifications, they produce falsehood. What, after all, makes an effective lie? It must be as close as possible to the truth to be convincing. It must also contain as small a proportion as possible of falsehood to truth so that the liar can keep the story straight and avoid self-contradiction. And finally, lies usually have to be produced on the spur of the moment, and it is a great aid to invention to have a stock of experiences on which to draw, as if they were conventional narrative themes. Odysseus's method makes sense, then, in regard to both the stories' production and their effect on their hearers. As lies, these tales are masterpieces.

Thus in his story to Athena he presents himself as devious, like Odysseus. He killed his Kretan enemy, he says, in ambush—Odysseus's typical mode of fighting in the *Odyssey* and a sign of his trickery (later the real Odysseus, with similar deceit, will kill the suitors, who, like the Kretan in this story, want to appropriate his possessions).[32] The Phoinikians correspond to the Phaiakians. Unlike them, the Phoinikians were blown off course and did not take Odysseus where he wished. We can observe where this motif originated and how it is transformed: though he has just learned from Athena that he really is on Ithaka, he thought at first that the Phaiakians deliberately deceived him and left him somewhere else. While he slept, he says, the Phoinikians unloaded his possessions and sailed away home—as the Phaiakians did. No wonder Athena is amused.

The basic device of the story Odysseus tells to Eumaios is duplication. He presents himself as someone other than Odysseus but one who has, like him, fought at Troy and has later undergone similar experiences. To prevent too close identification he describes himself as just the opposite in character:

> That was my element,
> war and battle. Farming I never cared for,
> nor life at home, nor fathering fair children.
> I reveled in long ships with oars.
>
> (14.222–24, p. 254)

And so the fictive persona got restless after being home a month from Troy, and the rest of his adventures, unlike the events they are modeled on, take place after, not before, the homecoming. The kernel of truth here might be Teiresias's prophecy that Odysseus will have to take one more journey before attaining peace at home. In any case the raid on Egypt is obviously based on the Kikones episode. The trusty Phoinikians of the story to Athena become the single treacherous Phoinikian merchant. The wreck of his ship by Zeus's thunderbolt, which only the narrator survives by clinging to the mast, replays the disaster that followed the eating of the Sun's cattle. The Kalypso episode, which ought to come next in some form, is omitted altogether, perhaps as too fantastic in a story aiming at verisimilitude, and the narrator floats on his mast to the Thesprotians, who perform the same function as the Phaiakians did for Odysseus but are an actual people in the northwest part of Greece, known to the Ithakans. There on the shore he meets the king's son (here a slight change from the Nausikaa episode, but recall Athena's disguise in Book 13), who clothes him and takes him home. The king took him in and sent him on his way to the island of Doulikhion, but in midsea the crew seized him and dressed him in rags, intending to sell him into slavery. He escaped when they landed for supper on Ithaka. This treachery is an intensified version of Odysseus's original suspicions of the Phaiakians; thus a story grows.

In Thesprotia, the beggar says, he heard news of Odysseus,

who also had been given hospitality by the king; Odysseus within the story therefore has the same experience as the *Odyssey's* Odysseus did with the Phaiakians. But this Odysseus has delayed his return to ask the oracle at Dodona (a famous oracle near the Thesprotians) whether he should return to Ithaka openly or in disguise. This bit of information is the essential message of the whole story: Odysseus will soon be home, and with great wealth. But there is also a playful hint that he may be in disguise. If Eumaios were to follow it up, he might consider the possibility that Odysseus and this stranger are the same person. Lying becomes exciting as Odysseus takes a risk. But Eumaios misses the point. In fact the story has on him exactly the effect Odysseus intends:

> Ah well, poor drifter,
> you've made me sad for you, going back over it,
> all your hard life and wandering. That tale
> about Odysseus, though, you might have spared me;
> you will not make me believe that.
> Why must you lie, being the man you are,
> and all for nothing?
>
> (14.361–65, p. 258)

Eumaios believes the whole story, except for the one thing that is true: that Odysseus will soon appear.

Odysseus's story to Penelope has two parts: the beggar's account of having entertained Odysseus in Krete on his way to Troy, together with the confirming description of the clothes he was then wearing, and his assurance of Odysseus's imminent return. As for the first, we know where Odysseus got the story of hospitality in Idomeneus's house; Eumaios fed it to him. He will believe no good news about his master, says the swineherd, as his hopes were raised by an Aitolian stranger and then disappointed:

> My master he had seen in Krete, he said,
> lodged with Idomeneus, while the long ships,
> leaky from gales, were laid up for repairs.
> But they were all to sail, he said, that summer,
> or the first days of fall—hulls laden deep
> with treasure, manned by crews of heroes.
>
> (14.382–85, p. 259)

Odysseus simply transfers this already fictional scene from the end of the Trojan War to the beginning, and changes the host from Idomeneus himself to his brother. He has had a forerunner, it seems, in this Aitiolian stranger who was Eumaios's guest and tells stories of Odysseus in Krete, and in others who Eumaios says have told similar tales to Penelope. This duplication, this time by the poet rather than by Odysseus, reinforces Odysseus's disguise by making him seem possibly just another opportunist. The characters—and by this time we the audience—have trouble distinguishing between Odysseus's genuine homecoming and its fictive counterparts.

In the other part of the story to Penelope Odysseus essentially repeats the tale about the Thesprotians and the inquiry to the oracle at Dodona. But now he tells about some of Odysseus's wanderings, not his own story based on them: the Cattle of the Sun, shipwreck, the Phaiakians. Again he omits Kalypso, as much this time out of tact in speaking to his wife as for plausibility. But the logic of the story would suggest that if he reached the Phaiakians Odysseus should already be home, and that would destroy the disguise. The beggar has come too close to telling the truth and now must take his Odysseus to the Thesprotians (who duplicate the Phaiakians):

> Long since he should have been here,
> but he thought better to restore his fortune
> playing the vagabond about the world;
> and no adventurer could beat Odysseus
> at living by his wits—no man alive.
>
> (19.282–86, p. 362)

It does not, of course, seem consistent with his desire for home to have Odysseus stay away like this. But the motive corresponds to the acquisitiveness we have seen in him; he told Alkinoos that he would stay with him for a year if doing so meant more gifts: "better far that I / return with some largesse of wealth about me" (11.355–59, p. 196).

For centuries many readers have been bothered by the notion of a hero who is a liar. That is to moralize inappropriately and also perhaps to impose alien standards on archaic Greek culture. These lies are manifestations of Odysseus's *metis*, that quality of con-

106

cealment and manipulation with which he and people in Mediterranean cultures even today face an unpredictable and potentially hostile world and survive in it (Winkler, 134–37). It is a good guess that Homer's contemporaries would have admired and enjoyed Odysseus's glibness. And so should we.

Whether Odysseus's lies deceive Penelope and more generally what her understanding of the situation is are difficult questions. To confront them we shall need to discuss Penelope more directly than before. She emerges in the later books of the *Odyssey* as a crucial actor in the plot, but at key moments Homer does not give full information about her thoughts and feelings.

Up until this point, although several scenes in Odysseus's house are punctuated by her descent from her upstairs quarters into the main hall, Penelope may seem vain and passive, given to naps and fits of weeping. A forceful statement of this view, one that says more about its author's attitudes than about Penelope, is given in a book published in 1909: "just the kind of woman who cries herself to sleep in difficulties, and wakes up looking wonderfully plump and fresh."[33] But there has not been much else for Penelope to do than bide her time and stave off the suitors. And in fact we have heard of her taking the initiative, the weaving and unweaving of the shroud for Laërtes. This admittedly is not purposeful activity, but it is not meant to be. Penelope resists the suitors with the means at her disposal: weaving in Homer is woman's quintessential activity. But weaving, taught to women by none other than Athena, not only signifies fidelity to the husband but also represents the feminine form of *metis* (also characteristic of *metis* is reversal, in this case the unweaving of what had been woven: Detienne and Vernant, 36–37). In the sense of "cunning plan" *metis* is something that in Homer's Greek can be woven, as when Odysseus asks Athena to weave him a *metis* ("weave me a way to pay them back" [13. 386 p. 242]). According to Greek society's division of labor, organization and care of the household were the wife's responsibilities, while the husband busied himself with external affairs: politics, warfare, the acquisition of possessions. Penelope's resisting *metis* in her own sphere is a perfect match for Odysseus's more active *metis* in his. Penelope turns to account what her society would see as her weakness and the strict limits on her (another definition of *metis*), and she thus preserves Odysseus's home for him.

Their reunion, which is a long, complex process that begins in Book 18 and culminates in Book 23, is an interplay of *metis* on the part of both. It is also the product of the poet's *metis*, indirect and full of delays. In this way Odysseus can test Penelope as well as others; her behavior and motives are what we now have to try to account for. But first, why is testing necessary? Why does Odysseus not simply go directly home and reveal himself to the wife for whom he has been longing all these years? Agamemnon has warned him against doing so, for his own murderous wife, he says, has given all women a bad name, even though he explicitly exempts Penelope from this condemnation (11.441–56, pp. 199–200). The same odd combination of ideas occurs in Book 13. Athena informs Odysseus of his wife's fidelity:

> And she? Forever
> grieving for you, missing your return,
> she has allowed them all to hope, and sent
> messengers with promises to each—
> though her true thoughts are fixed elsewhere.
> (13.379–81, p. 242)

But Odysseus replies that if Athena had not warned him of the suitors, "an end like Agamemnon's / might very likely have been mine." Klytaimnestra's example shows the kind of suspicion Penelope is exposed to (Murnaghan, 126–27), what might easily be thought of her by a male-dominated society given to categorizing women as dangerous and in need of control. We can thus appreciate all the more the dangers through which Penelope must thread her way and therefore the quality of her *metis* when she succeeds. As for Odysseus, such is his saving skepticism that he cannot rely solely on even Athena's words. He must see with his own eyes Penelope's worth, even though he knows it already.

The process begins in Book 18 with one of Penelope's descents into the hall. Here for the first time husband and wife set eyes on each other, though they never speak to each other directly. Instead Odysseus silently observes Penelope playing a role before their son and the suitors. In this first stage of their reunion, that is, he tests Penelope by watching her, and Penelope, although she probably does not know the scene has this significance, passes the test

108

triumphantly.

Athena puts the desire to appear before the suitors in Penelope "to set her beauty high / before her husband's eyes, before her son" (18.161–62, p. 341; the Greek text says "so that she should be more honored" in their regard). Penelope will gain stature in their eyes if they see that she is desirable to others—a hint of what this contest over a woman means to the men involved. Penelope experiences the desire as inexplicable, one that she can rationalize only by thinking of it as an opportunity to rebuke Telemakhos for associating with the suitors. There may be an element of flirtatiousness in Penelope—not to be taken seriously, and far outweighed by her love for Odysseus. If so, it shows how close this scene comes to turning into its opposite—proof to Odysseus of his wife's betrayal—if not for her good sense. At any rate there is no doubt of the effect of her beauty, specially enhanced by Athena, on the suitors: "their hearts grew faint with lust; / not one but swore to lie beside her" (18.212–13, p. 342; literally, their hearts were "enchanted"). When Eurymakhos compliments her beauty, Penelope replies that she is incomplete without Odysseus. She then tells of Odysseus's parting command to remarry if he is not home when the beard begins to grow on Telemakhos's cheek (18.257, p. 344), as has now happened. Despite her sorrow, the suitors are meant to be all the more aroused by the implied assurance that Penelope must soon marry one of them. Whether she has made up the story or not (we cannot tell), it may also express her own awareness that things are now reaching a climax, that she cannot postpone marriage much longer—and if so, that message is conveyed to Odysseus. Penelope proceeds to extort gifts from the suitors by reminding them that they are not wooing in the customary way (Homer is not entirely consistent on what is customary; some passages seem to reflect a dowry system, whereas others, like this one, assume presents and a "bride price" paid by suitors).

Odysseus appreciates what she is up to: "Odysseus' heart laughed when he heard all this— / her sweet tones charming gifts out of the suitors / with talk of marriage, though she intended none" (18.281–83, p. 345). Literally, "she was enchanting their hearts with honeyed words, though her mind was intent on other things." He admires her *metis*, which is like his, for elsewhere it is Odysseus who manipulates with honeyed words, who enchants the

Phaiakians and gets gifts from them with the story of his wanderings, and who is also masterful at saying one thing and intending
another. The last phrase in the quotation, "though she intended
none," is in Greek identical to Athena's assurance quoted earlier
(13.381, p. 242). Odysseus has confirmed Penelope's fidelity with
his own eyes.

Odysseus described to Nausikaa the ideal of marriage as "a
strong house held in serenity / where man and wife agree"
(6.183–84, p. 104)—literally, where they are "like-minded." In this
scene the complete like-mindedness of Penelope and Odysseus
begins to impress us (Winkler, 147), and this sense, which grows
stronger as the last books progress, is important in helping us keep
our bearings in the great scene in Book 19, in which husband and
wife talk together but still remain apart.

It is, of course, possible to say instead that "though she
intended none" represents only Odysseus's interpretation of Penelope's behavior and that in fact her motives are more complex, even
confused: love for her husband on the one hand, and, on the other,
uncertainty that he will ever return and the likelihood that she will
soon have to marry one of the suitors. Thus without betraying
Odysseus she wants to make the suitors woo her properly to prove
themselves worthy as potential husbands and pay her the tribute
she deserves. As Murnaghan (128–29) argues, it is one thing to
interpret this scene, as the text encourages us to do, from the perspective of the ending of the story and through our knowledge that
Odysseus is in fact home; it is another matter to view the situation
through Penelope's genuine uncertainty. From this perspective
Penelope's behavior still displays cleverness, only not in the way
Odysseus thinks it does, and the two are "like-minded" in that they
both possess an equal share of *metis*. A slight sign in favor of the
reading I have given is Athena's account of Penelope in Book 13,
but the uncertainty is genuine.

As Odysseus and Penelope test each other in Book 19, all the
important elements of a recognition scene are present: the expression of loss and longing by Penelope, her demand for tokens, their
production, and her acknowledgment of them (Murnaghan, 51–52).
Two displaced recognitions occur: of Odysseus by Penelope as he
was 20 years before, and of him now, not by Penelope but by
Eurykleia. Yet the scene does not end with an open recognition

between Odysseus and Penelope. Why not? Why does Odysseus not reveal himself to her? Why does Penelope, disregarding both the beggar's and her dream's assurances that Odysseus will soon be home, decide now to set the contest of the bow? Why, even after the suitors have been killed, is she reluctant in Book 23 to acknowledge him as her husband? One answer—by analyst critics—is that Book 19 in its present form represents an incomplete adaptation of an episode in earlier versions of the story in which an open recognition occurred and Penelope and Odysseus plotted the contest as a way to kill the suitors. That is in fact the version given by Amphinomos's shade (24.167–69, p. 450). Other answers are that Penelope secretly recognizes Odysseus[34] or that she does so unconsciously.[35] These attempts are all unsatisfactory—the first because it is desperate and leaves us with an incoherent text, and the other two because they raise questions of how far beyond the words of the text inference ought to go and because any recognition by Penelope now would ruin the wonderful scene of reunion in Book 23. A better answer is that Penelope suspects that the beggar might be her husband but cannot be sure (Winkler, 150–56). Let us, however, read the scene on the assumption that Penelope simply does not know, perhaps does not even suspect, and see where we get.

Penelope begins by asking Odysseus who he is (19.104–5, p. 356), and Odysseus, as he did in Book 7, tries to deflect the question, this time with a compliment. Penelope, he says, has won *kleos* like that of a king whose righteousness makes his land prosper (19.108–14, p. 357)—a strange comparison, as it casts her in a distinctively male role. Odysseus, I suggest, is testing her to discover her attitude toward control of the house, her "proper" role as wife, and her husband's absence. She replies,

> Stranger, my looks,
> my face, my carriage, were soon lost or faded
> when the Akhaians crossed the sea to Troy,
> Odysseus my lord among the rest.
> If he returned, if he were here to care for me,
> I might be happily renowned.
>
> (19.124–27, p. 357)

These are the words with which she answered Eurymakhos's compliment to her beauty (18.251–55, p. 344). In both places Penelope demonstrates loyalty to Odysseus; her refusal to contemplate the dominant role in the household complements her rejection of sexual attraction outside marriage. Here as earlier she acknowledges the void left by Odysseus. And so once again she meets a test without knowing she was undergoing it. Furthermore, in this same speech she tells him about her trick with weaving, evidence to him of both her loyalty and her *metis*.

Penelope (unlike Arete in Book 7) will not be put off: she ends the speech by again asking the beggar who he is. This leads to his account of his Kretan origin and the time he saw Odysseus there, which so reawakens his image in her mind that she weeps—and so does he, though internally, keeping his eyes dry. At this point might come a recognition, as in the later scene with Laërtes (24.315–26, p. 454). But instead she tests the beggar, by asking what clothes Odysseus was wearing then. The beggar's reply convinces her that he did see Odysseus and leads her to weep some more. His further story of having heard of Odysseus near home in Thesprotia might be all the more plausible to her. But like Eumaios, she cannot believe the one completely true thing he says, that Odysseus will soon be home—or she will not believe it. Her reply (19.309–16, p. 363) is ambivalent. She begins with a wish that his story might prove true, and then denies the possibility: "But my heart tells me what must be. / Odysseus will not come to me." Is this the overstatement and rhetorical self-dramatization common to characters in the *Odyssey* (Winkler, 137–38), or is Penelope, who we know from Eumaios has heard this kind of story before from imposters, defending herself from another disappointment by adopting the skepticism of *metis?* Either way, she does not necessarily disbelieve that Odysseus will come; she just cannot believe it. She will have to wait and see. In this context we might understand Penelope's own words about *kleos*, which balance those of Odysseus at the beginning of the scene (19.328–34, pp. 363–64): the harsh man will earn curses, but the kindly man widespread *kleos* (at issue is her treatment of the beggar). Here she herself is taking on a male role—the management of the house and hospitality—whereas she earlier refused one. She seems to be doing so by default and reluctantly, in the absence of Odysseus.

At this inconclusive moment Penelope seems about to draw the scene to a close by telling her maids to wash the beggar and prepare a bed for him. But it is continued, first by the episode of the scar and Eurykleia's recognition, which Odysseus himself inadvertently provokes when he asks that an old servant woman wash his feet. His own *metis* falters here. All through the long narrative of how Odysseus got the scar we are in suspense: what will Eurykleia do, having recognized Odysseus by the scar? Will Penelope find out after all? Homer seems to be playing with the conventions of recognition, seeing how close he can come to full recognition without pushing things quite that far, especially when Penelope commands Eurykleia, "bathe—bathe your master, I almost said, / for they are of an age" (19.357–58, p. 364). Unless we assume that Penelope has seen through the disguise, the scene excites by the way it threatens to plunge into premature recognition but finally retains its delicate balance (with the expedient of Athena momentarily distracting Penelope).

Here let us digress, as Homer does, and ask why else he has inserted this episode and left the scene with Penelope dangling to give a long account of how Odysseus got the scar. Eurykleia has played a role in it as Odysseus's nurse, so that the story becomes part of her recollection of Odysseus and thus an element in her recognition of him. More generally, it is fitting that as he sits in his hall with her and his wife, important episodes from his past critical to his identity should be recounted—how he got his name, acknowledgment in adolescence by his grandfather, and the boar hunt, which may be a means of initiation into manhood (recall the poem's concern with stages of life). At the same time Penelope is not involved in these incidents, since she is not a blood relative of Odysseus, and the story may imply the distance that remains between husband and wife, the need for further testing. In any case significant characteristics of Odysseus are defined in the narrative. Laërtes is oddly colorless here (just as he is absent from most of the *Odyssey*), and instead Odysseus's relation to his grandfather Autolykos is stressed. They share a certain quality; Autolykos (Lone Wolf), whose patron is Hermes (god of merchants and thieves among others), is distinguished for lies and swindles—*metis* at its least scrupulous. And the name he confers on the child commemorates Odysseus's relation with him: "odium and distrust I've won," says Autolykos, asked to name the child. "Odysseus should be his given name" (19.407–9, p. 366). *Odium* makes a good play on

Odysseus in English. More precisely, the name sounds like a Greek verb that means "be angry at, give pain to" (Athena exploits this association at the beginning of the poem when she asks Zeus, "What do you hold against [*ōdusao*] him now?" [1.62, p. 3]). Odysseus both suffers pain through most of the poem and inflicts it on others (the blinding of the Kyklops, the Phaiakians' punishment for conducting him home, the pain he is even now inflicting on Penelope). In his name Odysseus's two modes of relating to the world—active and passive—merge and become indistinguishable rather than contradictory (Peradotto, 133–34). George Dimock has stressed pain as basic to the *Odyssey*'s concern with humanity: to give and suffer pain is essential to human identity, relations with others, and "the sense of one's own existence."[36] The scar from the boar's tusk is an emblem of this pain, which is stressed during this approach to reunion between husband and wife and its postponement, painful to them both.

After this interlude Penelope keeps the scene going, in a different form. No longer is testing at issue. Instead Penelope asks the beggar for advice, or, perhaps more accurately, ratification of what is already clear to her, on two matters. First, she asks him to interpret her strangely self-interpreting dream (19.535–58, pp. 370–71), and when he does so in the only possible way, as a portent of Odysseus's killing of the suitors, she questions its truth in her famous speech on the two gates of dreams (19.560–69, p. 371). She makes it clear that she would like the dream to be true but seems (wisely) to prefer uncertainty to premature confidence. This skepticism amid assurance is a necessary prelude to her second request for advice, when she proposes the test of the bow for the next day.

Why she does so is perhaps not so puzzling after all, even on the assumption that she does not recognize Odysseus, or at most (with Winkler) suspects his identity. In Books 18 and 19 it is clear that Penelope senses that she has reached a critical time, when she can no longer keep the household running or stall the suitors in Odysseus's absence. The contest signifies this realization and is a way of forcing a conclusion. One of three things might happen. One of the suitors might string the bow and shoot through the ax heads, thus proving himself the equal of Odysseus—surely a remote possibility given their nature, but in that event perhaps it is time to admit that Odysseus never will come home and that she must

114

reconstruct her life without him. Or none of the suitors might succeed, in which case she will have fresh reasons for putting them off. Or Odysseus might come in time; the stranger has assured her that he will, in this short interval between the old moon and the new (19.306–7, p. 363), and she has seen some reason to trust him. Penelope is not giving up—just the reverse. She has to do something, and calculation of the probabilities shows that she has little to lose and everything to gain. She does what she can within the limits of her power: she contrives the *hora*, the time and the way in which events will reach a crisis.

That means that she takes an active role in the plot after all the years of waiting. Odysseus urges her to set the contest, for it will be his means of getting a weapon in his hands and killing the suitors. Penelope, then, gives Odysseus indispensable help in his triumph, which will thus be partly hers. Her active participation is more significant if she does not recognize him than if she does, for it shows that her action and his, taken on different grounds and from different perspectives on the situation, exactly match; his *metis* and hers complement each other. Their actions are independent but testify to their like-mindedness.

Penelope remains active in arranging the contest until a clearly marked point, when she urges the suitors to let the beggar try the bow (again aiding Odysseus's plan), and Telemakhos tells her that he will decide such things:

> Return to your own hall. Tend your spindle.
> Tend your loom. Direct your maids at work.
> This question of the bow will be for men to settle,
> most of all for me. I am master here.
> (21.350–53, p. 402)

Penelope has done the work of devising; now it is time for the physical contest—among men.

The contest of the bow brings out the real issues in the wooing of Penelope and Homeric men's striving for success generally. When Eurymakhos fails, he exclaims:

> Curse this day.
> What gloom I feel, not for myself alone,
> and not only because we lose that bride.

115

Women are not lacking in Akhaia,
in other towns or on Ithaka. No, the worst
is humiliation—to be shown up for children
measured against Odysseus—we who cannot
even hitch the string over his bow.
What shame to be repeated of us, after us!
(21.249–55, p. 399)

The issue in the suitors' wooing, then, is not so much Penelope herself as what possession of her will confer: standing in the eyes of other men. The successful one will have proved himself superior to the other suitors and equal to Odysseus. Conversely, failure will bring shame, characteristically expressed as consisting in what others will say. A Homeric man's activities usually involve competition with other men, and success always comes at someone else's expense. Status thus is finally achieved, if ever, only late in life (as with Nestor); until then it constantly needs to be won. These necessities also guide Odysseus. Although we may be sure of his love for Penelope, the shame of the suitors controlling the house and the deeper shame if one should succeed in supplanting him help to explain the violence of his revenge. As with the Trojan War (fought over Helen), the male competitive relationship is conducted here through the woman as intermediary. But Odysseus's own situation is paradoxical. Position in the household should be an exception to the general rule: once gained by succession from the father and made stable by marriage, it should not have to be tested and rewon. Furthermore, he is wooing again the woman to whom he is already married but is doing so violently.

A man hopes, of course, that his son will succeed him and that the son will prove equal to or better than his father, but these are supposed to happen at the proper time. Still, there is potential for competition between father and son (perhaps Laërtes is kept out of the way for most of the poem to avoid any hint of rivalry with Odysseus). Telemakhos's position on this score is interesting. His earlier-quoted rebuke to his mother echoes his words to her at 1.356–59 (quoted in Chapter 4), except that now "the bow" is substituted for "story-telling." Telemakhos's claim to authority now has considerably more force, although he is still his father's stand-in. He has grown up in the course of the poem and has been proving himself. Since Odysseus revealed himself to him in Book 16, Telemakhos has collaborated in the deception of the suitors and exerted considerable self-control. Essentially he has gone on acting the part that earlier was really his—that of the ineffectual adolescent—but does so now from a position of strength. In short, he has been initiated into his father's *metis*, as he will soon get his first taste of battle against the suitors.

Telemakhos is the first to try to string his father's bow (21.101–35, p. 395). Though the tone is playful, the moment is fraught with Oedipal tension as the son vies for his father's wife. Notice how this tension is defused. Three times Telemakhos tries and fails; the fourth time he would have strung the bow but "a stiffening in Odysseus" prevents him (in the Greek Odysseus explicitly signals a prohibition). The text has it both ways—Telemakhos can rival Odysseus but is not a threat to him—yet only because Telemakhos prudently accepts a secondary position. Sorting this issue out is a necessary prelude to the battle with the suitors.

The contest of the bow thus encapsulates the issues of male status underlying the impending fight. Having served as catalyst to the conflict, Penelope is absent while these stakes are decided. She reenters the action when, the suitors now dead, one step in Odysseus's homecoming remains: reunion with her. That reunion depends on her, and again she controls its timing and manner.

When Eurykleia comes to tell Penelope that the stranger is Odysseus and has killed the suitors, Penelope's response is ambivalent (23.1–84, pp. 429–31). She checks her joy with skepticism. This was, after all, one possible outcome of the contest of the bow, but only one. How can she be certain until she has seen with her own eyes, tested this man? She seems at once to know the truth and to guard against believing it. And so she goes downstairs and sits opposite Odysseus. Only the width of the hall divides them, but mentally they are still far apart. The ensuing scene will determine when and how husband and wife can cross the intervening space to each other's arms.

In a last display of adolescent impatience Telemakhos, unable to understand her reserve, rebukes his mother. She replies that she and Odysseus will know each other by "secret signs." Odysseus agrees and tactfully deflects his son's attention to a practical problem—how to keep word of the suitors' deaths from getting out too soon. What happens now will be between husband and wife; Tele-

117

makhos, who has twice told Penelope to stop interfering in matters that are men's concerns, has no place in this scene. An interlude follows in which Odysseus bathes. Athena makes him more handsome, as she did after his bath by the river in Book 6, and his appearance is described just as it was when he appeared to Nausikaa then (23.156–62, p. 434; 6.229–35, pp. 105–6). The repetition contrasts his possible marriage on Skheria with the marriage to which Odysseus has returned, the first a false version of the second. Now it is Odysseus who rebukes Penelope, as though to provoke her to test him as she intends. He gives her an opening by telling Eurykleia to make up a bed for him. Penelope seizes the opportunity to test him by his knowledge of the secret of their bed: immovable, built from the still-living trunk of the olive tree at the center of the house. Odysseus is furious at the thought that someone might have moved it. After so many triumphs of cleverness in the external world, he is finally outdone in *metis* by his own wife at home as she manipulates him in the interests of their marriage.

The bed is clearly a symbol of that marriage, a signifier of those values of the strong marriage that Odysseus expressed to Nausikaa. That marriage, like the olive tree, is the secret of the house's strength. Rooted in the earth, the tree, and through it the bed, is associated with the natural rhythms of birth, procreation, aging, and death. Odysseus describes his building of house and bed in some detail. As craftsman he has harnessed nature through a cultural act, but whereas in the Kyklops episode the division between nature and culture seemed unbridgeable, the olive tree as symbol seeks to reconcile them. The use of the olive tree for house and bed suggests culture building on but in harmony with nature.

And so Ithaka and this marriage come to stand for an ideal solution to this wider problem just when Odysseus is on the brink of consummating his reunion with Penelope. On hearing his speech about the bed she runs to him, embraces him, and addresses him by name for the first time:

> Do not rage at me, Odysseus!
> No one ever matched your caution! Think
> what difficulty the gods gave: they denied us
> life together in our prime and flowering years,
> kept us from crossing into age together.
> (23.209–12, p. 436)

Here as nowhere else we can understand what this 20-year separation has meant: a huge gap in their life together, when they might have enjoyed watching their infant son grow to adulthood. Although nothing can cancel the pain, the text also gives a sense of a relationship that has endured so steadfastly through the like-mindedness of the partners that this wonderful moment of reunion is achieved and the future ensured. Penelope goes on to explain her defensive skepticism (also for the first time) and uses Helen as an example of the danger of headlong action and excessive trust without calculation of risks. Helen, she says, was the cause of her and Odysseus's woes—woes through which they have come by virtue of their separate but mutual loyalty and their intelligence.

Odysseus shares her joy and the release of candor, now finally possible:

> Now from his breast into his eyes the ache
> of longing mounted, and he wept at last,
> his dear wife, clear and faithful, in his arms,
> longed for
>   as the sunwarmed earth is longed for by a swimmer
> spent in rough water where his ship went down
> under Poseidon's blows, gale winds and tons of sea.
> Few men can keep alive through a big surf
> to crawl, clotted with brine, on kindly beaches
> in joy, in joy, knowing the abyss behind:
> and so she too rejoiced, her gaze upon her husband,
> her white arms round him pressed as though forever.
>   (23.231–40, p. 436)

As a description of Odysseus's feelings, the simile evokes the time when Odysseus literally came to shore after Poseidon's blows in Book 5 and allows us to appreciate that moment in retrospect as ensuring the reunion that has now taken place. More generally, it sums up the importance of homecoming as continued life by opposing it to a watery death. But in a way unique for Homeric similes these lines simultaneously describe something else too—Penelope's feelings—as we are surprised to find when we reach their end ("and so she too rejoiced"). Applied to her the simile involves a reversal of roles and suggests that Penelope, without moving from Ithaka, has undergone the same kinds of experiences and survived the same kinds of perils as Odysseus on his wanderings. If we look back to the event from which this simile arises, we find that Odysseus, reaching shore, is described, by a similar kind of transposition, as a son who sees his father revive (5.394–99, p. 92). And when Telemakhos returns to Ithaka, Eumaios's joy on seeing him is compared to that of a father whose only son has returned from a 10-year absence, while Odysseus, whose only son Telemakhos actually is, remains in the background unrecognized (16.17–21, pp. 289–90). And yet he, the father, is the one who has long been away and is now restored to the son. All these "reverse similes" that punctuate moments of restoration emphasize the interdependence of the three family members and, once again, the like-mindedness of Odysseus and Penelope.[37]

The reunion is fittingly commemorated when they go to bed together and tell each other their hardships (Odysseus, true to his name, tells of the pain he both gave and received [23.306–7, p. 439]). Yet even now there is a dissonance. Just before this point, right after they first embrace, Odysseus tells of the further journey Teiresias has prophesied that he must take. The present moment is not final reunion and peace but another stage on the way to that point. The end of the story is ensured but postponed, even beyond the end of the poem.

Where the *Odyssey* does end is a hard question. Since the Alexandrian period, many scholars have considered all or parts of everything after the point when Odysseus and Penelope go to bed (23.296, p. 438), including all of Book 24, post-Homeric additions. The arguments are not conclusive, however, and whoever composed the disputed passages, they add significantly to the text as we have it. They deserve attention.

The scene among the dead in Book 24 is the counterpart of the one in Book 11. The shades of the same heroes reappear here (Thornton, 5), but Odysseus does not. Instead of needing a way home, he is there, and whereas the dead have only the past to contemplate, he has just accomplished another great deed. Akhilleus commiserates with Agamemnon on the ignominy of his death; the elaborate contrast with Odysseus is once again important. On the other hand, Agamemnon congratulates Akhilleus on his happy fate: death in battle, fierce fighting over his corpse, a glorious funeral to commemorate his greatness, and a conspicuous tomb to keep his fame alive. This fate is the consummation of the hero's purpose, and we note again how traditional heroism assumes death as its outcome. At this moment enter the shades of the suitors, evidence of Odysseus's latest achievement and continued life and thus of how he surpasses other great heroes. Now he is the one Agamemnon congratulates after hearing Amphimedon's story:

> O fortunate Odysseus, master mariner
> and soldier, blessed son of old Laërtes!
> The girl you brought home made a valiant wife!
> True to her husband's honor and her own,
> Penelope, Ikarios' faithful daughter!
> The very gods themselves will sing her story
> for men on earth—mistress of her own heart,
> Penelope!
> Tynadareus' daughter waited, too—how differently!
> Klytaimnestra, the adulteress,
> waited to stab her lord and king. That song
> will be forever hateful. A bad name
> she gave to womankind, even the best.
>
> (24.192–202, p. 451)

Like male heroes, Klytaimnestra and Penelope are both envisioned as subjects of song and are contrasted through the kind of song each will get. Penelope's faithfulness will stand out against the background of the suspicion usually accorded women (the result, Agamemnon claims, of acts by the likes of Klytaimnestra). Penelope has earned *kleos*, the result of her *arete* or "excellence" (another catchword of heroism); a woman shares in the achievement and renown usually reserved in epic poetry to men. Moreover, Odysseus's own *kleos* depends on Penelope, whereas in the *Iliad* the interests and outlook of men and women sharply diverge. Agamemnon's glory depended on his wife too. In the interplay between these couples' stories we see at once a broader scope of action allowed to Greek women than is usual and a reflection of Greek culture's deep ambivalence about them.

Odysseus has been able to stay with Penelope only until dawn. He still must face the suitors' relatives, and leaves house and town for the countryside and Laërtes. Odysseus's treatment of his father has long disturbed readers by its apparent cruelty. Why does he bother to spin yet another tall story, which reduces Laërtes to abject grief, when directness can hold no danger? One answer is that reunions in this poem are always preceded by testing and by eliciting the feelings of the person tested, and that may be valid. But we should not abolish the problem by driving a wedge between theme and feeling. Uneasiness at this scene is appropriate. The value of *metis*, we remember, is ambiguous, and here we may see its darker, inconsiderate side. In any case it is important that the tokens of identity Odysseus offers Laërtes are not only his scar but also the fruit trees that Laërtes gave him as a child (24.331–44, p. 455). They enable the old man to go back in memory to the time when he himself was the figure of authority and Odysseus the dependent (Murnaghan, 31), and this glimpse of the past reconstructs for us another of Odysseus's relationships. At the same time, the saplings' growth to maturity parallels Odysseus's own and is a reminder that his original relation with his father is now reversed: he is now in possession. Along with Odysseus's restoration to home, of which this is the final stage, Laërtes must also be reconstructed and reintegrated in an old man's proper role.

This reconstruction occurs when Laërtes (whose form Athena has filled out [24.367–69, p. 456]) arms to fight the suitors' relatives and the men of three generations of this family—Laërtes, Odysseus, and Telemakhos—stand together in armor. This tableau is all the more significant in view of epic tradition's depiction of the heroic ideal as passed on from father to son. When Laërtes exclaims, "Ah, what a day for me, dear gods! / to see my son and grandson vie in courage!" (24.514–15, p. 461), he reflects the competition, even (or especially) within a family, that heroism entails, the rivalry that cannot be wholly suppressed. In the abortive battle that follows, Laërtes is the one who kills an opponent (fittingly Eupeithes, whose name means "glib persuader" and who has stirred up the relatives and is the father of Antinoos, the suitors' ringleader). Before Laërtes sinks back into old age's feebleness, his warrior might flowers momentarily once again.

Battle fury flares up in Odysseus as well, and in defiance of Athena's command he chases the retreating foe. He is too prudent, however, to be carried away entirely, and when Athena, prompted by Zeus's thunderbolt, again tells him to stop, he obeys. Thus Odysseus's last acts in the poem show his two sides, the warrior and the man of self-control, as though they were still not finally reconciled even when final peace is about to be achieved. And then the poem ends, with Athena arbitrating a settlement—an abrupt and contrived ending that opens out into continued life in peace and prosperity but seems unsatisfactory nevertheless.

Or perhaps when the real end is so far in the future and so long deferred, and at the same time when there is nothing to narrate from this point on, the only appropriate conclusion is one that draws attention to its own inconclusiveness.

8

Poetry in the Odyssey

The *Odyssey* is an enormously self-conscious text; it constantly draws attention to and reflects on its nature and function as a poem, and especially as an epic poem that uses a certain set of conventions, presents a certain kind of heroism and associated values, and stands in a particular relation (not wholly conforming) to its tradition. Poetry therefore comes to stand for many of the things that the *Odyssey* is about.[38]

Poetry, that is, as the archaic Greeks conceived it. According to this notion, which is implicit in several texts, the poet is inspired by the Muses. They give him not a state of ecstatic vision and not primarily particular words but knowledge of stories, the deeds of gods and mortals, in both past and present, and perhaps also the typical themes by which to shape a narrative. These last might include type scenes, such as hospitality and sacrifice, and also motifs that might be infinitely recombined to narrate, say, the death of a hero or his return home. In one sense, then, the Muses stand for the tradition. As daughters of Zeus, they are intermediaries between mortals and gods; they extend the normal range of human knowledge, for the poet and through him for the audience, to the doings of gods, human history, and contemporary events elsewhere on the earth. Thus Odysseus, who is in a position to know, compliments Demodokos, who cannot have firsthand knowledge, on the accuracy of his Trojan stories, which Odysseus attributes to the Muse or Apollo (8.488–91, pp. 139–40). The Muses' mother is Mnemosyne,

"Memory." In an essentially oral culture publicly performed poetry maintains knowledge of the past and also preserves the culture's dominant worldview and values, which it may also hold up to scrutiny and criticism. Our texts, therefore, often refer to poetry as "remembering." As a way of ordering experience and knowing the world, poetry is usually said to produce "delight" or even "enchantment" in its hearers.

The *Odyssey* contains several scenes of poetic performances, which must mirror the way this text itself was originally performed: the lines sung, or at least chanted, to the accompaniment of a plucked stringed instrument, forerunner of the later lyre. Such descriptions, then, call attention to the *Odyssey* as a text and raise questions about its purpose and effect on the audience. These poems-within-the-poem have a double focus: on the internal narrative, which resembles or contrasts with the surrounding text, and on the responses of the internal audience, which often raise the question of poetry's relation to actual experience.

Poetry becomes a theme at the beginning, when Phemios sings the Returns and Penelope asks him to stop. Telemakhos in effect tells her that she does not understand poetry. Zeus, not poets, is to blame for the Akhaians' woes, and "men like best / a song that rings like morning on the ear" (1.351–52, p. 12). These words are often taken as expressing the prevailing aesthetic: people like to hear the latest songs. But this ignoring of content for novelty, this divorce of poetry from experience, is put on the lips of an inexperienced youth. Immediately afterward Telemakhos claims authority in the house, yet he has had the experience neither to back up this claim nor to judge poetry. His response to the song brands him as charmingly naive. The suitors, for their part, take delight. This conventional response is especially appropriate for them, since they are taking advantage of the most prolonged and arduous of the Returns. The unusual response, however, is Penelope's weeping. It has a parallel in the equally remarkable tears of Odysseus in Phaiakia as he hears Demodokos's stories of his own exploits at Troy—another sign of this couple's like-mindedness, separated though they are by such distance. Odysseus's weeping is especially paradoxical, since to hear his fame celebrated during his lifetime should be the fulfillment of an epic hero's aspirations.

Perhaps they weep because they are personally involved in

126

these narratives; "aesthetic distance" such as the Phaiakians enjoy is necessary for pleasure in poetry. This explanation is insufficient, however, since in Book 23 Odysseus and Penelope take delight in telling their stories to each other. What Odysseus and Penelope have in common before then is that they are still undergoing their experiences and do not know what the end will be, and that is what makes stories of personal import painful. From the perspective of the ending a story can be understood and evaluated as a whole, and sense can be made of it as part of the order of the world. This temporal distance is what enables a narrative of even painful events to give pleasure. When Eumaios, for example, is about to tell his own very mixed experience, he says,

> Here's a tight roof; we'll drink on, you and I,
> and ease our hearts of hardships we remember,
> sharing old times. In later days a man
> can find a charm in old adversity,
> exile and pain.
>
> (15.398–401, p. 280)

Literally he says, "let us take delight in each other's mournful woes, remembering them." Memory in the form of narrative can be reconstructive, then. For individuals who share stories informally or for a society that hears epic poetry, it is a way of making sense of experience.

Telemakhos has told Penelope in Book 1, "story-telling will be men's concern," but he is again wrong. The *Odyssey* shows how narrative becomes this woman's concern, as she helps to shape the poem's plot while living it. And so it is not with Telemakhos but with Penelope that Odysseus shares stories in the culmination of all the poem's internal narratives, when man and wife lie in bed together (23.300–43, pp. 438–40). These are tales of suffering, as the text emphasizes, but having reached at least this provisional conclusion, both can take pleasure in them. Together they retell much of our *Odyssey*. In Chapter 6 we noticed how the poem's narrative is constantly catching up with itself as episodes are recounted first as they happen and then by a character in the poem as past. Here Odysseus tells Penelope of his wanderings, but now in chronological order, with the Phaiakians as well as Kalypso now in the past. Earlier he told the Phaiakians how he recounted to

127

Aiolos his wanderings up to that point. Narrative nests within narrative, and all are contained within our *Odyssey* (if we ignore for the moment the inconclusive ending). Odysseus's story grows longer and more elaborate with the passage of time. As we read we experience events as they occur and then observe them become the past, objects of memory for the characters within the poem. Up to this point, however, there has always been a distance between the poem and its internal narratives. But Odysseus's narrative to Penelope abolishes this distance, and with it the *Odyssey* presents itself as a poem in the process of ending, taking its place among other poems. Through its self-conscious transformation of present into past, it suggests the proper mode of our response: pleasure in pain overcome and coherence snatched from the flux of human life.

The *Odyssey* reflects not only on narrative and its effects in general but also on particular narratives. We have noticed how often it appropriates other heroic stories, many if not all told in other epic poems, in order to distinguish itself as superior to them. Thus the Returns in general, when Phemios sings them, are called a "bitter song"; nevertheless, Odysseus's Return will be a triumph. As an occasion for *kleos* beyond the glory he won at Troy and as a transition to a happy life with Penelope, it outdoes even the relatively successful Returns of Nestor and Menelaos. Odysseus is also contrasted with other heroes from Troy in Books 11 and 24. Agamemnon's *kleos* is canceled by the manner of his death. Akhilleus fares better: his *kleos* is intact, for he died on the battlefield. But Odysseus comes out best of all, for in addition to his fame as a warrior he gets the kind of *kleos* that comes from surviving. Thus the *Odyssey* presents its subject as more vital than those of other epics, its hero as superior to even the greatest of other heroes, Akhilleus, who has glory because he is dead.

In large part that claim is based on Odysseus's qualities. Although much has been said of his *metis*, still another aspect of it is also a sign of the *Odyssey*'s self-consciousness: the presentation of Odysseus as a double of the poet.

In his long narrative to the Phaiakians in Books 9–12 Odysseus "replaces" the poet. The Kikones episode, with its reduction of sacking cities to self-defeating brutality, may be a reflection on stories about Troy such as Demodokos has just sung twice in Book 8, with the suggestion that the very different kind of story that Odysseus tells is superior. In Book 11 (11.330–32, p. 195) Odysseus does something characteristic of a performing poet: he stops in midstory to see if his audience is tiring, but (perhaps because he has cleverly stopped at an exciting place, the middle of his account of the dead) he is urged to go on. Demodokos too has paused and been urged to continue (8.87–92, p. 127). In addition, the effect of Odysseus's story on the Phaiakians is twice said to be enchantment (11.334, p. 195; 13.2, p. 229)—conventionally the effect of poetry. And in the interlude of Book 11 Alkinoos draws an explicit comparison of Odysseus to a poet (though, as we shall see, his assumption of that as a guarantee of truthfulness is naive and perhaps grows out of the Phaiakians' pleasure in narrative without the corresponding experience): "You speak with art, but your intent is honest. / The Argive troubles, and your own troubles, / you told as a poet would, a man who knows the world" (11.367–69, p. 197).

Odysseus's lies on Ithaka are also like poetry. Just as he manipulates, transforms, combines, and recombines a stock of themes, so a poet in this tradition varies a limited stock of typical motifs and scenes to produce constantly new stories.[39] Homer in the *Odyssey* similarly repeats and manipulates motifs and patterns of action in endlessly varying contexts. The key to the lies' success—their closeness to the truth—is an achievement of a poet as well. "We know how to tell lies that resemble the truth [*idmen pseudea polla legein etumoisin homoia*]," say the Muses in Hesiod's *Theogony* (27–28), "and we know how, when we want, to utter true things." The description of Odysseus's lies to Penelope in Greek resembles the first of these clauses: "now all these lies he made appear so truthful [*iske pseudea polla legôn otumoisin homoia*] / she wept as she sat listening" (19.203, p. 360). Eumaios in fact tells Penelope about the effect of the beggar's lies (as we know them to be):

There was no end to what he made me hear
of his hard roving; and I listened, eyes
upon him, as a man drinks in a tale
a minstrel sings—a minstrel taught by heaven
to touch the hearts of men. At such a song
the listener becomes rapt and still. Just so
I found myself enchanted by this man.

(17.517–21, p. 328)

129

The analogy between Odysseus and a poet expresses many of his qualities—his intelligence, his verbal cleverness, his values as a man of culture (the singer is one of the craftsmen listed by Eumaios at 17.381–87, p. 323). But it also again suggests his superiority as an epic hero, in line with the *Odyssey*'s other claims for its subject. Usually in heroic epic certain outstanding men and women act, whereas others—poets—preserve and spread their *kleos* through narrative song but are not themselves active. Although warriors and the poems about them intimately depend on each other, song, as an element of peacetime culture, is likely to be viewed in battle contexts as a pursuit of the weak and effeminate (e.g., *Iliad* 3.52–55). This attitude is paradoxical inasmuch as heroic action in war would be pointless without poetry, and the essence of warrior ideology would be undermined. It points, however, to a larger problem that deeply vexes Homeric heroes: how to reconcile word and deed, peace and war. If a hero exists for action and constantly risks his life in order at least to die gloriously, then for all his splendor he is one-sided. Odysseus's heroism, though it includes that of the warrior, is presented as much more comprehensive through the comparison of him to a poet.

The right time (*hora*) for speech and for action is in fact a theme of the poem. The Sirens, for instance, offer Odysseus a song about Troy and knowledge of all that happens on earth. All the allure of poetry tempts Odysseus, but on their island meadow amid a windless sea, surrounded by the rotting bones of wayfarers who stopped to hear them, the Sirens are dangerous to him. If he too stopped, the story about himself that he is creating by living it would end, and since the Sirens offer poetry cut off from the human society to which it is central, no one would hear of him. This poetry, here and at this time, would mean death in its worst aspect, oblivion —exactly the opposite of its usual purpose. Odysseus must still strive, and poetry must find its rightful place in his world.[40] At Alkinoos's palace, on the other hand, there is an interlude in action that allows time for speech about the past, and Odysseus shows that he can both act and spread the *kleos* of his deeds himself. Staying here permanently, however, would end his story prematurely: action would be devalued in favor of word.

On Ithaka, as Odysseus bides his time, words—his lies—again replace action. Or, rather, they become a kind of action, as they serve his plan, so that word and deed begin to converge. They come together fully at the climactic moment when Odysseus strings his bow:

> But the man skilled in all ways of contending,
> satisfied by the great bow's look and heft,
> like a musician, like a harper, when
> with quiet hand upon his instrument
> he draws between his thumb and forefinger
> a sweet new string upon a peg: so effortlessly
> Odysseus in one motion strung the bow.
> Then slid his right hand down the cord and plucked it,
> so the taut gut vibrating hummed and sang
> a swallow's note.
>
> (21.406–11, p. 404)

Here, as he embarks on his greatest triumph, Odysseus the warrior and Odysseus the poet are one.

In this depiction of Odysseus we can detect the *Odyssey*'s comment on the tradition of heroic epic, especially as represented by the *Iliad*. There the heroic ideal is expressed as "to be a speaker of words and a doer of deeds" (*Iliad*, 9.443), yet almost no one in that poem displays this balance of talents, except, perhaps, for Odysseus. The *Iliad*'s chief hero, Akhilleus, is "the best of the Akhaians" in battle, but though he can reflect on courage, death, and the reasons for fighting, he is not a "speaker of words" in the way Odysseus is, in the ability to manipulate the world for his purposes through language. Of himself Akhilleus admits that no one can match him in battle, "though others are better in the assembly" (*Iliad*, 18.105–6). Once, it is true, Akhilleus plays the lyre and sings "the fames of men"—an epic poem (*Iliad*, 9.186–89). But at that point Akhilleus has withdrawn from fighting in anger at Agamemnon: for Akhilleus, song can only replace action. He cannot combine them, or control both word and deed, the way Odysseus can. The *Odyssey*, then, implicitly claims that, even on the *Iliad*'s own terms, Odysseus, not Akhilleus, is the consummate hero.

The *Iliad*, however, celebrates Akhilleus's kind of heroism. The *Odyssey* incorporates Akhilleus, pays tribute to his qualities, but shows why he is dead and Odysseus alive. If the *Odyssey* takes a polemical stance toward its tradition, that is partly due to the com-

131

petitive nature of poetry as of much else in Greek life (Edwards, 11–13). But the effect (as Edwards also argues) is to emphasize that this poem presents its own set of values within that tradition: praise of heroic action that risks death but wins life because its hero also prizes peace, community with others, and all those things the poem associates with civilization. He is comfortable within human limits. The *Odyssey*, by calling attention to itself as a poem and thus as the construction of pleasurable memory out of pain, and through the poet's association of himself with his hero, becomes as it unfolds an emblem of those values. It is a semblance and simultaneously a re-creation of civilized order in the world.

9

Unraveling the Web

The *Odyssey*, through its hero and through its exploration of a series of polarities that we have subsumed under the contrast between nature and culture, shows how much is possible within the limits on human life. In scope it ranges comprehensively throughout the unknown and the ordinary human worlds. Its sympathy includes but extends beyond the narrow range of male warrior heroism and encompasses activities, objects, and people associated with peace, from the most lowly to the highest social level. There are, however, aspects of the poem that escape this formulation and that seem to work against a wholly determinate meaning.

Consider class, for example. We would expect a king who undergoes humiliation disguised as a beggar and who explores his society through all its classes from the perspective of an outsider to discover the inequities of the social structure. Moreover, in the sympathetic portrayal of some common people we would expect to find the suggestion that quality cuts across class boundaries, that what matters is a person's nature rather than social role. Neither of these things in fact happens. The Phaiakians are presented as an ideal polity, but when Alkinoos suggests to his nobles a further round of gifts for Odysseus, he says something that inadvertently reveals his social assumptions: "Let each man add his tripod and deep-bellied / cauldron: we'll make levy upon the realm / to pay us for the loss each bears in this" (13.13–15, p. 229).

In other words, the expense of the aristocratic system of gift exchange, the cement of heroic society, is borne by the lower classes. What is wrong on Ithaka is not portrayed as systemic; it is simply that the king is absent. Odysseus as king is said to have been as gentle as a father (2.47, p. 20); although kings can be unfair, says Penelope, Odysseus never wronged anyone (4.687–93, p. 73). His restoration, then, is an ideal solution to the problem, opened up by the suitors' behavior, of the well-born exploiting the lowly. With a gentle father back at its head, the hierarchically organized society can flourish; the hierarchy itself is not finally questioned but, rather, affirmed. As for the portrayal of commoners, in Philoitios we find the naturally good man, and in Melanthios, Melantho, and the rest a picture of the lowly corrupted by evil masters, the suitors. But these are minor characters. Eumaios, who is the outstanding portrait of devotion and kindness, turns out to be the son of a king, Ktêsios, whose name means "Rich in Possessions" (15.413–14, p. 281). His qualities are those considered to be inherited within the nobility.

It is not clear whether the *Odyssey* is defending kingship, which was then threatened by an increasingly powerful aristocracy (who would be represented by the suitors)[41] or whether it adopts the outlook of an aristocratic warrior class headed by a king whose interests are identical with theirs (the suitors then would violate aristocratic norms, but these would remain intact). Either way, the system by which those at the top of society are maintained by the labor of those below is upheld. The poem seems to open up questions about it but then closes them off with the ideal solution of the return of the righteous king, whose rule makes the people and all of nature flourish (19.107–14, p. 357).

Something similar happens in the case of gender. Penelope has an independence and importance rarely accorded women in Greek literature or (as far as we can tell) Greek life. The text emphasizes her like-mindedness with Odysseus and their marriage as collaboration between them. But just where the patriarchal social structure seems to be loosened and subversive thoughts of equality allowed, control is reasserted. We have seen that in Books 18 and 19 Penelope declines a controlling role and emphasizes instead her dependence on Odysseus, and that her *kleos* in fact arises from her loyalty to her husband (Book 24). The limits on her as a woman are broadened but never abolished; she finally is a worthy partner to her husband but subordinate to him. A counterexample of too much female independence is Helen, whose initiative in running off with Paris caused the whole Trojan War. Within the *Odyssey* she still shows signs of "excessive" independence, when she preempts Menelaos in recognizing Telemakhos (4.116–46, pp. 56–57) and in interpreting the bird omen on the young man's departure (15.169–78, p. 273). Penelope shares the equivocal position of Alkinoos's wife, Arete, through whom the kingship comes to Alkinoos and whom Odysseus is advised by Nausikaa and Athena to supplicate but who then takes little part in giving hospitality to Odysseus. In fact when Arete claims the status of host she is told bluntly by her husband that *he* has the power in the house (11.336–53, p. 196), in words identical with Telemakhos's claims to Penelope concerning Phemios's song and the bow in Books 1 and 21.

Odysseus himself is in some respects an ambivalent figure, because of the very comprehensiveness of his character. Opposing qualities are not wholly harmonized within him. We have already commented on the ambiguous nature of *metis* as both constructive intelligence and dangerous duplicity, and on the pain he inflicts as well as suffers wherever he goes, often as a result of saving himself with his cleverness. In the Kyklops episode we saw that this ambivalence is the ambiguity of culture itself, as the Kyklopes are presented both as being savage, the antitype of culture, and as escaping the categories of "nature" and "culture" through the identification of their environment with the Golden Age. In this latter sense the man of culture disrupts the harmony of their life. The symbolism of the bed (Book 23) cannot wholly paper over this contradiction within cultural values. In this same episode we noticed a tension in Odysseus between the *metis* by which he escapes from the Kyklops and the heroic pride that makes him shout his true name to Polyphemos. But *metis* and pride are roughly equivalent to the word and deed that Odysseus, as the text suggests by comparing him to a poet, reconciles in an exemplary way.

The parallel opposition that Odysseus seems to mediate, between the man of peace and the warrior, remains similarly problematic. The simile comparing him to a singer as he strings the bow, which in one sense expresses his combination of these roles, is in another sense deeply incongruous. Song belongs with the feast as a sign of peace and civility. There is all the difference in the world between the lyre and the murderous bow. With similar violent incongruity, the murder of the suitors takes place at and disrupts a feast. Antinoos is shot as he lifts the wine cup to his lips—shot through the gullet, appropriately enough, in view of his gluttony. But for all his guilt, the narrative here directs sympathy to him with an odd pathos: "the cup was in his fingers: / the wine was even at his lips: and did he dream of death? / How could he?" (22.10–14, p. 409). As he falls he upsets the table, spilling the food into the dust—a mark of the disruption of civilization. Aigisthos, we recall, killed Agamemnon at a feast—a circumstance that makes the deed seem an upheaval of civilized order. It is, on the one hand, poetic justice that Aigisthos's counterparts, the suitors, are killed in the same setting. On the other hand, it makes Odysseus's deed uncomfortably similar to his. Odysseus, to be sure, is acting to restore civility amid chaos, but is it possible to separate completely the goal from the means? The battle with the suitors brings the violence of Iliadic warfare into the center of civilization, a hall meant for feasting, hospitality, and, at most, song about such deeds. Odysseus's revenge cannot escape the taint of savage violence; the text seems to want to keep warfare and peace separate but does not wholly succeed. From this perspective it is appropriate that the poem's ending preserves the tension between these two sides of Odysseus unresolved when peace is at hand but, filled with battle fury, he rushes on the suitors' relatives.

And finally there is the narrative itself, certain features of which raise questions about the reality of its story. In the way the narrative is always catching up with itself as the present continuously turns into the past to be recounted later, the text not only raises the important issue of memory and its uses but also makes time, achievement, and the very notion of life in the present seem elusive. Odysseus is a hero with a past and a constantly deferred future. Even such moments as his reunion with Penelope are transitory; he has to leave her again the morning after their first night together in 20 years, just as he will have to leave her to take his final journey. Moreover, if Odysseus in his lies is like a poet, then a poet can be a liar. The very thin line between his tales and his narrative to the Phaiakians (which is at least purportedly true) confuses our sense of the distinction between fiction and truth—in a way consistent with Greek ideas about poetry as represented in the claim by Hesiod's Muses to tell lies resembling truth as well as truth. This confusion is heightened by Eumaios's (true) story, which suspiciously resembles fiction (15.390–484, pp. 280–83). The Phoinikian nurse and traders there play the same treacherous role as the Phoinikian adventurer in Odysseus's lying tale to Eumaios, and the nurse, like that fictive adventurer, is killed by Zeus's thunderbolt. When truth and lies are merely variations of each other, what makes the one real and the other false? How do we tell the difference? Furthermore, we noticed that Odysseus's lies carefully excluded the fantastic episodes of his supposedly real wanderings. Eumaios was born in a place with the same character as the scene of Odysseus's adventures; it has strongly marked features of the Golden Age. And so what passes for truth in this poem seems like fantasy, whereas lies contain no monsters or miracles but are indistinguishable from the reality of experience. Which are we to believe?

Thus the *Odyssey*, like its hero, is a polytropic text, impossible to reduce to a single summary or a set of oppositions. It is structured, in a way typical of early Greek thought, on a series of polarities—nature versus civilization, war versus peace, action versus word, force versus *metis*. But these polarities are not finally stable; the opposite terms interpenetrate, and whole areas of experience escape them altogether. The text tries to control and mediate them. To an extent it succeeds, but not completely, and the signs of only partial success are evident in what evades or goes against the dominant meaning.[42] As the poem simultaneously achieves meaning and partly undermines it, does it show us how civilization must accommodate all the violence and irrationality at large in the world and within the human psyche, give us a vision of what that would be like, and yet, by confusing its own claims to truth, cast doubt on the possibility of such balance and control? And if so, doesn't the *Odyssey* become an even more interesting text than if it were simpler?

notes

1. Anthony Snodgrass, *Archaic Greece: The Age of Experiment* (Berkeley and Los Angeles: University of California Press, 1980), 64–65; hereafter cited in text.

2. J. N. Coldstream, *Geometric Greece* (New York: St. Martin's Press, 1977), 303–15; hereafter cited in text.

3. Chester G. Starr, "The Decline of the Early Greek Kings," *Historia* 10 (1961): 129–38.

4. The discovery in 1980 at Lefkandi in Euboea of a warrior's burial (strongly reminiscent of a Homeric hero's burial) and, next to it, the grave of a woman with gold ornaments, both beneath a large apsidal building and all dated to the second half of the tenth century, may lead to a drastic revision in the chronology of all the developments discussed in this chapter. Because the implications have not been drawn, however, I have presented the current scholarly consensus on these matters.

5. M. I. Finley, *The World of Odysseus* (New York: Viking Press, 1978); hereafter cited in text.

6. On the general characteristics of *metis*, see Marcel Detienne and Jean-Pierre Vernant, *Cunning Intelligence in Greek Culture and Society* (Atlantic Highlands, N.J.: Humanities Press, 1978), 11–26; hereafter cited in text.

7. John Peradotto, *Man in the Middle Voice: Name and Narration in the Odyssey* (Princeton, N.J.: Princeton University Press, 1990), 119; hereafter cited in text. Peradotto identifies the first view with myth and the "centripetal" language of Bakhtinian theory and the second with Märchen or fairy tales and Bakhtin's "centrifugal" language.

8. For this chapter I have ransacked Howard Clarke's *Homer's Readers: A Historical Introduction to the "Iliad" and the "Odyssey"* (London and Toronto: Associated University Presses, 1981) and W. B. Stanford's *The Ulysses Theme: A Study in the Adaptability of a Traditional Hero*, 2d ed. (Ann Arbor: University of Michigan Press, 1968), both of which are hereafter cited in text; also Rudolf Pfeiffer, *History of Classical Scholarship: From the Begin-*

nings to the End of the Hellenistic Age (Oxford: Clarendon Press, 1968). Although I have added some points of my own, my debt to these works, for both facts and generalizations, is extensive.

9. W. Rhys Roberts, trans., Longinus "On the Sublime," 2d ed. (Cambridge: Cambridge University Press, 1935), 67; hereafter cited in text.

10. The Divine Comedy: Inferno, trans. Charles S. Singleton (Princeton, N.J.: Princeton University Press, 1970), 26.112–20.

11. Norman Austin: Archery at the Dark of the Moon: Poetic Problems in Homer's Odyssey (Berkeley, Los Angeles, and London: University of California Press, 1975), 87–88. See especially his Chapter 5 (pp. 239–53).

12. Bernard Fenik, Studies in the Odyssey (Hermes Einzelschriften 30 [Wiesbaden: Franz Steiner Verlag, 1974]), 208–27; hereafter cited in text. Fenik points out a number of similarities between the episodes of the Kyklops and the Cattle of the Sun.

13. These lines are omitted from Fitzgerald's translation, as they were thought by ancient scholars much later than Homer to have been interpolated. The grounds for this suspicion are weak, and the lines are important to the depiction of Telemakhos and to gender issues in the poem. I have given a literal translation here. Readers of Fitzgerald's translation should mentally supply them on p. 12 between the lines "Others, how many others, lost their lives" and "the lady gazed in wonder and withdrew."

14. For more information on the Epic Cycle, see Richmond Lattimore, trans., The Iliad of Homer (Chicago: University of Chicago Press, 1951), 24–28.

15. Compare W. S. Anderson, "Calypso and Elysium," in Essays on the "Odyssey": Selected Modern Criticism, ed. Charles H. Taylor, Jr. (Bloomington: Indiana University Press, 1963), 77; hereafter cited in text.

16. Ovind Andersen, "Odysseus and the Wooden Horse," Symbolae Osloensis 52 (1977): 5–18.

17. The Basic Works of Aristotle, ed. Richard McKeon (New York: Random House, 1941), 1129.

18. Charles Paul Segal, "The Phaeacians and the Symbolism of Odysseus' Return," Arion 1 (1962): 17–64; hereafter cited in text.

19. A similar contrast appears with equally powerful effect in the Iliad, 22.147–56: Akhilleus, about to kill the Trojan leader Hektor, chases him past two springs, one of hot and the other of cold water, with stone washing pits where Trojan women used to wash clothes in peacetime, before the Akhaians came.

20. I owe a general debt to Fenik's discussion of this scene, Studies in the Odyssey, especially 53–56.

21. Walter Burkert, "Das Lied von Ares und Aphrodite" (The Song of Ares and Aphrodite), Rheinsiches Museum 103 (1960): 142.

22. See Ann L. T. Bergren, "Odyssean Temporality: Many (Re)turns," in

Notes

Approaches to Homer, ed. Carl A. Rubino and Cynthia W. Shelmerdine (Austin: University of Texas Press, 1983), 50–54; hereafter cited in text. I wish to acknowledge a general debt to this article in my discussion of time and narrative, although I have taken Bergren's ideas in somewhat different directions.

23. George DeF. Lord, "The *Odyssey* and the Western World," in Taylor, ed., 43–44.

24. Compare Segal, 45, with notes 31 and 41, and Seth L. Schein, "Odysseus and Polyphemus in the *Odyssey*," *Greek, Roman, and Byzantine Studies* 11 (1970): 75–76.

25. Norman Austin, "Odysseus and the Cyclops: Who Is Who," in Rubino and Shelmerdine, eds., 22–30.

26. On the pun, see Anthony J. Podlecki, "Guest-Gifts and Nobodies in *Odyssey* 9," *Phoenix* 15 (1961): 130–31, and Schein, 79–80.

27. The uneasy coexistence of these qualities is brought out by Rainer Friedrich, "Heroic Man and *Polymetis*: Odysseus in the *Cyclopeia*," *Greek, Roman, and Byzantine Studies* 28 (1987): 121–33.

28. Gregory Nagy, *The Best of the Achaeans: Concepts of the Hero in Archaic Greek Poetry* (Baltimore and London: Johns Hopkins University Press, 1979), especially 42–58.

29. Sheila Murnaghan, *Disguise and Recognition in the "Odyssey"* (Princeton, N.J.: Princeton University Press, 1987), 20–26. On testing, see also Agathe Thornton, *People and Themes in the "Odyssey"* (Dunedin, New Zealand: University of Otago Press, 1970), 47–51. Both sources are hereafter cited in text.

30. Jenny Strauss Clay, *The Wrath of Athena* (Princeton, N.J.: Princeton University Press, 1984), 186–212.

31. John J. Winkler, *The Constraints of Desire: The Anthropology of Sex and Gender in Ancient Greece* (New York: Routledge, 1990), 135; hereafter cited in text.

32. Anthony T. Edwards, *Achilles in the "Odyssey,"* Beiträge zur klassischen Philologie 171 (Meisenheim: Anton Hein, 1985), 32–33, 35–38; hereafter cited in text.

33. F. M. Stawell, *Homer and the "Iliad"* (London, 1909), quoted in W. B. Stanford, *The Odyssey of Homer*, 2d ed. (New York: St. Martin's Press, 1967), 1:230 (on 1.346 ff.).

34. Philip W. Harsh, "Penelope and Odysseus in *Odyssey* XIX," *American Journal of Philology* 71 (1950): 1–21.

35. Anne Amory, "The Reunion of Odysseus and Penelope," in Taylor, ed., 100–21.

36. George Dimock, "The Name of Odysseus," in Taylor, ed., 72.

37. See Helene P. Foley, "'Reverse Similes' and Sex Roles in the *Odyssey*," *Arethusa* 11 (1978): 7–26.

141

38. The role of poetry and broader issues of language in the *Odyssey* have been much discussed, most recently by Simon Goldhill, "Language and Representation in the *Odyssey*," in *The Poet's Voice: Essays on Poetics and Greek Literature* (Cambridge: Cambridge University Press, 1991), 1–68.

39. James M. Redfield, "The Making of the *Odyssey*," in *Parnassus Revisited*, ed. A. C. Yu (Chicago: American Library Association, 1973), 148–49.

40. See the excellent discussion of the Sirens and of *kleos* generally in Charles Segal, "Kleos and Its Ironies in the *Odyssey*," *L'Antiquité Classique* 52 (1983): 22–47, reprinted in Harold Bloom, ed., *Homer's the "Odyssey,"* Modern Critical Interpretations (New York and Philadelphia: Chelsea House, 1988).

41. S. G. Farron, "The *Odyssey* as an Anti-Aristocratic Statement," *Studies in Antiquity* 1 (1979–80): 59–101.

42. For this point approached in a different way, see Ann L. T. Bergren, "Helen's 'Good Drug': *Odyssey* IV 1–305," in *Contemporary Literary Hermeneutics and Interpretation of Classical Texts*, ed. Stephen Kresic (Ottawa: University of Ottowa Press, 1981), 517–30.

bibliography

PRIMARY WORKS

Fagles, Robert. *Homer: The Iliad.* New York: Viking Press, 1990. With introduction and notes by Bernard Knox.

Fitzgerald, Robert. *Homer: The Iliad.* New York: Doubleday, 1974.

____. *Homer: The Odyssey.* New York: Vintage Classics, 1990.

Lattimore, Richmond. *The Iliad of Homer.* Chicago: University of Chicago Press, 1951 (frequently reprinted).

____. *The Odyssey of Homer.* New York: Harper & Row, 1965.

Lawrence, T. E. *T. E. Lawrence's Translation of Homer's Odyssey,* edited by Bernard Knox. Oxford: Oxford University Press, 1991.

Mandelbaum, Allen. *The Odyssey of Homer.* Berkeley: University of California Press, 1990.

Pope, Alexander. *The Odyssey of Homer,* edited by Maynard Mack. Twickenham Edition of the Poems of Alexander Pope, vols. 9–10. New Haven, Conn.: Yale University Press, 1967.

Shewring, Walter. *The Odyssey.* Oxford: Oxford University Press, 1980.

Stanford, W. B. *The Odyssey of Homer.* 2d rev. ed. London: Macmillan, 1967. Greek text with introduction and notes.

SECONDARY WORKS

Books

Atchity, Kenneth, ed. *Critical Essays on Homer.* Boston: G. K. Hall, 1987.

Austin, Norman. *Archery at the Dark of the Moon. Poetic Problems in Homer's "Odyssey."* Berkeley: University of California Press, 1975.

Bloom, Harold, ed. *Homer's the "Odyssey."* New York and Philadelphia: Chelsea House Publishers, 1988.

Clarke, Howard. *Homer's Readers: A Historical Introduction to the "Iliad" and the "Odyssey."* London and Toronto: Associated University Presses, 1981.

Clay, Jenny Strauss. *The Wrath of Athena: Gods and Men in the "Odyssey."* Princeton, N.J.: Princeton University Press, 1983.

Dimock, George E. *The Unity of the "Odyssey."* Amherst: University of Massachusetts Press, 1989.

Edwards, Anthony T., *Achilles in the "Odyssey,"* Beiträge zur klassischen Philologie 171. Meisenheim: Anton Heim, 1985.

Edwards, Mark W., *Homer, Poet of the "Iliad."* Baltimore: Johns Hopkins University Press, 1987.

Goldhill, Simon. *The Poet's Voice: Essays on Poetics and Greek Literature.* Chapters 1 and 2. Cambridge: Cambridge University Press, 1991.

Griffin, Jasper. *Homer on Life and Death.* Oxford: Clarendon Press, 1980.

_____. *Homer: The "Odyssey."* Cambridge: Cambridge University Press, 1987.

Katz, Marylin A., *Penelope's Renown: Meaning and Indeterminacy in the "Odyssey."* Princeton, N.J.: Princeton University Press, 1991. This book appeared too late for me to use it in my own discussion.

Luce, J. V. *Homer and the Heroic Age.* New York: Harper & Row, 1975.

Murnaghan, Sheila. *Disguise and Recognition in the "Odyssey."* Princeton, N.J.: Princeton University Press, 1987.

Peradotto, John. *Man in the Middle Voice: Name and Narration in the "Odyssey."* Princeton, N.J.: Princeton University Press, 1990.

Rubino, Carl A., and Cynthia W. Shelmerdine, eds. *Approaches to Homer.* Austin: University of Texas Press, 1983.

Snodgrass, Anthony. *Archaic Greece: The Age of Experiment.* Berkeley and Los Angeles: University of California Press, 1980.

Steiner, George, and Robert Fagles, eds. *Homer.* Englewood Cliffs, N.J.: Prentice-Hall, 1962.

Stanford, W. B. *The Ulysses Theme: A Study in the Adaptability of a Traditional Hero.* 2d ed. Oxford: Basil Blackwell, 1963.

Taylor, Charles H., Jr. *Essays on the "Odyssey": Selected Modern Criticism.* Bloomington: Indiana University Press, 1963.

Thornton, Agathe. *People and Themes in Homer's "Odyssey."* London: Methuen, 1970.

Vivante, Paolo. *Homer.* Hermes Books. New Haven, Conn.: Yale University Press, 1985.

_____. *The "Iliad": Action as Poetry.* Boston: Twayne Publishers, 1991.

Winkler, John J. *The Constraints of Desire: The Anthropology of Sex and Gender in Ancient Greece.* New York and London: Routledge, 1990. Chapter 5 is on Penelope.

Articles

Amory, Anne. "The Reunion of Odysseus and Penelope." In *Essays on the "Odyssey": Selected Modern Criticism,* edited by Charles H. Taylor, Jr., 100–121. Bloomington: Indiana University Press, 1963.

Bibliography

Anderson, William S. "Calypso and Elysium." In *Essays on the "Odyssey": Selected Modern Criticism,* edited by Charles H. Taylor, Jr., 73–86. Bloomington: Indiana University Press, 1963.

Austin, Norman. "Odysseus and the Cyclops: Who Is Who?" In *Approaches to Homer,* edited by Carl A. Rubino and Cynthia W. Shelmerdine, 3–37. Austin: University of Texas Press, 1983.

Bergren, Ann L. T. "Odyssean Temporality: Many (Re)Turns." In *Approaches to Homer,* edited by Carl A. Rubino and Cynthia W. Shelmerdine, 38–73. Austin: University of Texas Press, 1983.

____. "Helen's 'Good Drug': *Odyssey* IV 1–305." In *Contemporary Hermeneutics and Interpretation of Classical Texts,* edited by Stephane Kresic, 201–14. Ottowa: University of Ottowa Press, 1981.

Dimock, George E., Jr. "The Name of Odysseus." In *Essays on the "Odyssey": Selected Modern Criticism,* edited by Charles H. Taylor, Jr., 54–72. Bloomington: Indiana University Press, 1963.

Foley, Helene P. "'Reverse Similes' and Sex Roles in the *Odyssey.*" *Arethusa* 11 (1978): 7–26.

Harsh, Philip W. "Penelope and Odysseus in *Odyssey* XIX." *American Journal of Philology* 71 (1950): 1–21.

Lord, George DeF. "The Odyssey and the Western World." In *Essays on the "Odyssey": Selected Modern Criticism,* edited by Charles H. Taylor, Jr., 36–53. Bloomington: Indiana University Press, 1963.

Schein, Seth L. "Odysseus and Polyphemus in the *Odyssey.*" *Greek, Roman, and Byzantine Studies* 11 (1970): 73–83.

Segal, Charles Paul. "*Kleos* and Its Ironies in the *Odyssey.*" In *Homer's the "Odyssey,"* edited by Harold Bloom, 127–49. New York and Philadelphia: Chelsea House Publishers, 1988.

____. "The Phaeacians and the Symbolism of Odysseus' Return." *Arion* 1 (1962): 17–64.

index

Agamemnon, murder of, 32, 42,
43, 68–69, 91, 108, 120–21,
128, 136
age groups, 37–40, 52–53
Agora, 4, 6, 57
Aias, son of Oileus, 43
Aias, son of Telamon, 16, 93
Aigisthos, 32, 136
Aiolos, episode of, 70, 74–78,
127–28
Aithiopes, 50, 72
Akhilleus, 10–11, 91–93, 120–21,
128, 131–32
Alexandrian scholarship, 17–18,
23, 25–26, 120
Alkinoos: asserts power in the
house, 135; naïveté of, 129;
Odysseus received by, 56,
58; Odysseus questioned by,
59; palace of, 57. See also
Phaiakians
allegory, 17, 21–22
alphabet, Greek. See writing
analysts, 23–24, 111
Antikleia, mother of Odysseus,
68, 89, 90
Antinoos, 100, 122, 136
Ares and Aphrodite, song of, 34,
62
Arete: equivocal position of, 135;
Odysseus received by, 56,
58; Odysseus questioned by,

58–59. See also Phaiakians
Argos 96
Aristarchus, 17
aristocrats: and hero cults, 7;
kings replaced by, 6, 134;
represented by suitors, 134;
self-awareness of, 6
Aristotle: Homeric Problems, 17;
Poetics, 17, 21, 66; Politics,
49
Artemis, 53
assembly, 35. See also Agora
Athena, 122–23; metis of, 98–99;
Odysseus aided by, 57–58,
98–100, 118; Odysseus's
lying story to, 98, 102–3,
103–4; sends Telemakhos to
Pylos and Sparta, 38–39;
visits Telemakhos, 36
Atlas, 50
Autolykos, 113

Basileus, 6
bed, marriage, 74, 118, 135
beggars, 100–1. See also belly;
eating; food; Odysseus
belly, 57, 101
bow, contest of, 111, 114–17

cannibalism: of Kyklops, 74, 76,
79, 82–83, 102; of
Laistrygonians, 75, 77, 79;

of Skylla, 75; suitors'
behavior similar to, 102. *See
also* eating; food
class, 6, 100, 133–34
colonization, 4, 7–8, 81
competition, 115–17, 122; poetry
and, 131–32
crafts, 4, 85. *See also*
shipbuilding
culture: ambivalence of, 80–81,
87; hospitality central to,
100–2; poetry as expression
of, 132; vs. nature, 12,
72–80, 102, 118, 135, 137;
vs. nature in Kyklops
episode, 80–88. *See also*
crafts; *metis*; shipbuilding

Dante, *Divine Comedy*, 19–20,
26, 89, 91
dares, 19
Dark Age, 3, 5, 6, 7, 25
Dead, visit to (Book 11), 68–69,
78, 88–93
Dead, second scene of (Book 24),
120–21
death, nature of, 88–90
Delos, 55
Demodokos, songs of, 34, 61–63,
125, 126, 128, 129
Dictys of Krete, 19
Dodona, 105, 106
Dorian invasion, 3

eating, theme of, 35–36, 74–75,
78. *See also* cannibalism;
feasting; food
Eidothea, 98
Eighth-Century Renaissance, 3–6
Elpenor, 68, 90
Elysium, 43, 48, 50, 57
enchantment, effect of songs and
lies, 75, 109, 126, 129

Epic Cycle, 40–41, 63, 66, 93
epic poetry. *See* poetry
Eratosthenes, 25–26
Eumaios, 120, 127; hospitality
of, 96; life story of, 137;
noble birth of, 134;
Odysseus's lying story to,
102–3, 104–5; response of to
Odysseus's tale, 105, 112,
129; skepticism of, 105–6
Eupeithes, 122
Euripides: *Hekabe*, 16; *Kyklops*,
16
Eurykleia, 112–14
Eurymakhos, 115

fate, 33
father/son relations, 116–17,
122
feasting, 61, 83, 135–36; Aiolos
and, 74–75; between mortals
and gods, 49–50; scenes of,
36–37, 61; significance of,
35–36. *See also* hospitality;
sacrifice
food, 49–50, 79, 101. *See also*
feasting; belly; cannibalism

gender, 134–35; division of labor
by, 107; issue of in hearing
poetry, 127; in Nausikaa
episode, 53–56; relation of to
kleos and song, 121; roles
determined by, 111–12;
stereotypes of, 108. *See also*
Penelope; bow, contest of;
competition
Gigantes, 57, 58
gods: hospitality protected by,
101; justice vs. arbitrariness
of, 32–34; mortals
distinguished from, 49,
56–57, 72; separation of

mortals from, 49–51. *See also* sacrifice

Golden Age, 49–50, 57, 87, 135, 137

guest gift, 36, 83, 102. *See also* hospitality

Helen, 116, 119; adultery of, 34; independence of, 135; relations of with Menelaos, 43–45; worshiped as heroine, 7

Helios. *See* Sun, Cattle of

Herakles, 91

Hermes, 47–48; 89, 98, 113

Hermione, 43

Herodotus, 15

hero cults, 6–7

heroism: contradictions in, 130; and death, 91–93, 120–21; *Odyssey*'s definition of, 10–11, 91–93, 131–32; transmitted from father to son, 122; vs. peace, 63, 130, 135–36; vs. prudence, 83–84, 87–88; word and deed in, 39, 130–31. *See also* competition

Hesiod, 15; *Theogony*, 50, 129, 137

home, value of, 10–11, 48–49, 60–61, 79–80

Homeric epics: audiences of, 8, 15; composite society in, 7–8; influence of on subsequent culture, 7, 9, 15; and oral poetry, 7

hora (timeliness), 31, 97, 115, 130

Horace, *Ars Poetica*, 21

hospitality, 74–76, 125; religious significance of, 101–2; rules of, 36, 59; social significance

of, 56–57; suitors' abuse of, 36, 101–2. *See also* feasting, guest gift, Kyklops

house, of Odysseus, 95–96, 102, 118

household, in Homeric society, 34–35

Idomeneus, 103, 105–6

Iliad, 53, 66, 140n19; *Odyssey*'s relation to, 10–11, 18–19, 131–32

Ithaka: relation of to scenes of Odysseus's wanderings, 72, 99–100; state of in Odysseus's absence, 34–35, 40, 90, 96, 100, 134. *See also* home

Joyce, James, *Ulysses*, 9, 26

Kalypso, 10; affinity of with sea, 50; characterization of, 60–61; disregards rules of hospitality, 60; episode of (Book 5), 31, 47–50, 60, 66–67, 73–74, 76, 78, 104, 106, 127; name of, 49

Kazantsakis, Nikos, *Odyssey*, 26

Kharybdis, 74, 78

Kikones, episode of (Book 9), 71–72, 73, 76, 104, 128–29

kingship, 6, 134

Kirke, 71; episode of (Books 10, 12), 75–78; prophecies of, 68

kleos (fame), 45, 51, 60, 61, 63, 69, 87, 92, 121, 128; defined, 39; and poetry, 130

Klytaimnestra, 32, 108, 121

Krete, 24, 105–6, 112

Kyklopes: characterization of, 80–81; island near the coast of, 7–8, 80–81; Phaiakians

and, 57, 58; relation of to
nature, 80–81, 82, 135
Kyklops: blinding of by
Odysseus, 33; curse of, 68,
88; episode of (Book 9), 71,
76–77, 80–88, 135; Golden
Age affinities of, 87;
hospitality inverted by,
82–83, 101, 102; pastoral
nature of, 80, 86–87;
relation of to sea, 74. *See
also* cannibalism

Laërtes, 38; colorlessness of,
113, 116; Odysseus's
reunion with, 112, 121–22;
reconstruction of, 122
Laistrygonians, 98, 99; episode of
(Book 10), 33, 75, 77. *See
also* cannibalism
Lefkandi, 139n4
lies. *See metis*; Odysseus; poetry
Linear B, 24
Livius Andronicus, 18
"Longinus," *On the Sublime*,
18–19
Lord, Albert, 25
Lotos Eaters, episode of (Book 9),
73–74, 76

marriage: ideal of, 55, 110, 118;
social importance of, 36,
52–53, 76
Megapenthes, 43
Melanthios, 134
Melantho, 134
memory, 67, 69, 70, 125–26,
127–28, 132
Menelaos, 35–36, 98; fate of in
Elysium, 43; Helen's
relations with, 43–45;
hospitality of to Telemakhos,
39–40; return of from Troy,

41–43; worshiped as hero, 7
metis, 86, 137; ambivalence of,
122, 135; and culture, 12,
82, 84–86; definition of, 12,
106–7; and lies, 98–99,
102–3, 106–7; of *Odyssey*
poet, 86, 108. *See also*
Odysseus; Penelope
Milton, John, 9
Mnemosyne, 125–26
muses, 125–26, 129, 137
Mycenaean period, 3, 6–7, 24, 25

narrative, 9–10, 96–97; fiction
and truth in, 136–37; first
and third person in, 67,
69–71; inconclusiveness of,
123; incorporation of other
stories in, 40–46, 63, 128;
time in, 65–69, 127–28, 136
nature: in Kyklops episode,
80–88; vs. culture, 12,
72–80, 102, 118, 135, 137
Nausikaa, 98, 110, 118;
depiction of, 52–53; episode
of (Book 6), 52–56, 104;
possible marriage of to
Odysseus, 55–56, 59–60,
118
Nektar and Ambrosia, 49, 74
Nestor, 35–36, 39, 116; admires
Telemakhos, 39; Return of
from Troy, 41–42
New Criticism, 26–27
Nostoi, 41
Nymphs, Cave of, 99

Odysseus: acquisitiveness of,
106; affinity of with Athena,
98–99; ambivalent qualities
of, 12–13, 72, 84, 87–88, 93,
122–23, 135–36;
comprehensiveness of as

hero, 130–31; conflict within between heroism and prudence, 83–84, 87–88; contrasted with Agamemnon, 42, 43, 91, 120–21; contrasted with Akhilleus, 91–93, 120–21, 131–32; death of, 40, 69, 90; declines immortality, 48–49; delays revelation of name, 58, 61, 111–12; desire for home of, 10, 48–49, 60; disguise of as beggar, 45, 97, 99, 100–102; disguise of as Outis, 85–86; essential qualities of, 11–13, 93; folly of, 71, 81–82, 87–88; gentleness of as king, 134; Helen's and Menelaos's reminiscences of, 44–45; heroic side of, 61, 62, 83–84, 87–88, 135; house of, 95–96; *kleos* of, 42, 45, 60, 91–92, 121, 128; learns from wanderings, 71; like-mindedness of with Penelope, 109, 115, 119–20, 126; lies of, 102–7, 129, 130–31, 136–37; *metis* of, 12, 48, 56, 58–59, 82, 84 86, 91, 92, 97, 98–99, 102, 106, 109–10, 113, 128; name of, 113–14; others' memories of, 37; narrates wanderings (Books 9–12), 69–70; poetlike qualities of, 86, 128–31, 135; post-Homeric depictions of, 16–17, 18, 19–21, 26; relation of to culture, 80–81, 82; reunion of with Laërtes, 121–22; reunion of with Penelope, 108–20; as "sacker

of cities," 72, 87–88; scar of, 113–14, 122; Telemakhos's potential rivalry with, 117; weeps at Demodokos's songs, 61–63, 126–27; word and deed reconciled by, 131; worshiped as hero, 7. *See also* Penelope; recognition, Antikleia

olive wood, 52, 74, 85, 118
Olympos, scenes on, 34, 47
omens, 96–97
oppositions, polar, 72–73, 79–80, 133, 137
oral poetry, 7, 23–25, 36
Orestes, 32
Outis, 85–86, 88

Paris, adultery of, 34
Parry, Milman, 23–24
Penelope: dream of, 114; *kleos* of, 111–12, 121, 134; like-mindedness of with Odysseus, 110, 115, 119–20, 126, 134; loyalty of, 32, 111–12, 134–35; *metis* of, 107–8, 109–10, 112, 115, 118; Odysseus's lying story to, 102–3, 105 6, 112; preferred to Kalypso by Odysseus, 48; relation of to suitors, 109–10; relation of to Telemakhos, 37–38, 115, 116, 117–18; relative independence of, 134–35; response of to Odysseus's lies, 112; reunion of with Odysseus, 108–20; role of, 107, 115, 117; skepticism of, 112, 114, 117, 119; uncertain motives of, 110–11, 114–15; weaving of, 31, 107, 112; weeps at

Phemios's song, 41, 126–27.
See also gender; Odysseus;
recognition
Phaiakians: characterization of,
57–58, 60–61, 62, 78; and
class exploitation, 133;
episode of (Books 6–8),
39–40, 52–63, 73, 75, 78,
99, 105, 106, 127–28, 130,
133; position of in narrative,
67–68; reception of
Odysseus by, 56–63; as
transitional stage for
Odysseus, 51–52. *See also*
Alkinoos; Arete; Nausikaa
Phemios, song of, 37, 41, 126,
128
Philoitios, 134
Phoinikians, 4, 103–4, 137
Pindar, 16
Plato, *Ion*, 15
Plutarch, 21
poetry: effect of, 126–28; function
of, 69; Greek view of,
125–26; opposition of to war,
130; performance of, 126;
performances of within
Odyssey, 126–27; related to
lies, 129, 136–37. *See also*
Demodokos; enchantment;
lies; Phemios
polis, 4
Polyphemos, meaning of, 88. *See*
Kyklops
Polytropos, 11–12
Pope, Alexander, 22–23, 84
Poseidon: dines with Aithiopes,
50; persecutes Odysseus,
12, 32–33, 50, 57, 82, 88
poststructuralism, 27
Prometheus, 50
Proteus, 43
Pylos, decorum of, 35–36, 40

quarrel between ancients and
moderns, 21

recognition: pattern of, 97;
scenes of, 97–100, 110–14,
121–22; testing in, 97, 100,
122; testing of each other,
by Penelope and Odysseus,
107–14, 117–18
Returns, narratives of, 41–46,
126, 128
rhapsodes, 15

Sack of Ilium, 45
sacrifice, 36, 50, 75, 125. *See
also* feasting
Schliemann, Heinrich, 24
Scholia, 17
Seneca, *Trojan Women*, 18
Shakespeare, William, *Troilus
and Cressida*, 20–21
shipbuilding, 80, 81, 85
similes, reverse, 51, 119–20
Sirens, episode of (Book 12), 75,
78, 130
Skheria, 51
Skylla, episode of (Book 12), 70,
75, 76, 78. *See also*
cannibalism
Sophocles: *Ajax*, 16; *Philoktetes*,
16
Sparta, decorum of, 35–36, 40
Stoic philosophers, 17, 18
structuralism, 27
suitors: Aigisthos parallel to, 32,
136; as aristocrats, 134;
arrogance of, 97; crimes of,
34–35, 96, 101–2, 134;
Penelope's effect on, 109;
response of to poetry, 126;
violation of norms by, 36–37,
109. *See also* hospitality

Sun (Helios), Cattle of: and
causality, 33; episode of
(Book 12), 74–75, 78, 99,
104, 106; position of in
narrative, 68

Teiresias, prophecy of, 68–69, 90,
104, 120
Telegonia, 40
Telemakhos, 31, 120; adolescent
qualities of, 38, 117–18,
126; attitude of to Penelope's
remarriage, 38; cannot
receive guests, 36–37;
journeys to Pylos and
Sparta, 34, 35, 38–40;
maturation of, 37–40,
116–17; Orestes parallel to,
32; as potential rival of
Odysseus, 117; relation of to
Penelope, 37–38; views
about poetry of, 126
temples, 5, 57
Tennyson, Alfred Lord, *Ulysses*,
26
testing. *See* recognition
Theocritus, 16
Theoklymenos, 36–37
Thesprotians, 104–5, 106, 112

time. *See* narrative
trade, growth of, 4–5
Trojan Horse, 45, 62–63
Trojan War: cause of, 34;
Odyssey's perspective on,
41, 62–63, 71–72, 128–29
type scenes, 36, 125, 129
tyrants, 6

Unitarians, 23–24

vase painting, 5
Ventris, Michael, 24
Virgil, *Aeneid*, 9, 18, 88–89

warfare, 53, 63, 71–72
weaving, relation of to *metis*, 107.
See also Penelope
wine, 83
Wolf, F. A., 23
writing, 5, 7, 23–25

Xenophanes, 15, 17

Zeus: deceived by Prometheus,
50; as father of the Muses,
125; pronounces on mortal
folly, 32–33; as Xenios, 101
Zoilus ("Scourge of Homer"), 17

the author

William G. Thalmann, professor of classics at the University of Southern California, has taught at Yale University and Hobart and William Smith Colleges. He is the author of *Dramatic Art in Aeschylus's "Seven against Thebes," Conventions of Form and Thought in Early Greek Epic Poetry*, and articles on Greek tragedy and Homer.